THE PARSIS
A CLASSIC COLLECTION

THE PARSIS
Martin Haug

THE PARSI RELIGION
John Wilson

ZOROASTRIANISM
Rustom Masani

ZOROASTRIANISM

THE RELIGION
OF THE GOOD LIFE

ZOROASTRIANISM

THE RELIGION
OF THE GOOD LIFE

BY

SIR RUSTOM MASANI
M. A.

WITH A FOREWORD BY

John McKenzie

INDIGO BOOKS

AN
INDIGO BOOK
PUBLISHED BY INDIGO BOOKS
Paperback division of
COSMO PUBLICATIONS,
24-B, Ansari Road, Darya Ganj,
New Delhi 110 002, India.

INDIGO BOOKS and
COSMO PUBLICATIONS
are wholly owned subsidiaries of
GENESIS PUBLISHING PVT. LTD.,
New Delhi, India

ZOROASTRIANISM.
THE RELIGION OF THE GOOD LIFE

First INDIGO Edition 2003

ISBN 81-292-0049-x

PRINTED AND BOUND IN INDIA

FOREWORD

My friend Mr. R. P. Masani has produced a little book on Zoroastrianism which should be of great value to all who wish to know something of the social and religious background of the Parsi people. There are many who have this desire, for though the Parsi people are few in number—so few that in the statistics of world population they are simply insignificant—they have an importance that is out of all proportion to their numbers. They are the best educated community in the whole of Asia. In trade, commerce, and industry they have proved themselves among the most active and enterprising of the peoples of the world. In public spirit and philanthropy they have set a notable example to all men. Exiled for many centuries from their own land, they have maintained their identity as a race, and they have not ceased to take pride in their long and wonderful history. It is a just pride, for in all their history there is nothing more surprising, and nothing that more truly shows the quality of this people, than the fact that a mere remnant of little over a hundred thousand should have maintained their national consciousness, and should have carried into their life in the modern world so much of the spirit that animated their great ancestors in the days of the ancient Persian Empire.

In these days they are not without their troubles and anxieties, but it is characteristic of them that they are their own most unsparing critics. In this fact we find ground for hope that their future will be no less distinguished than their past has been.

I shall not here say anything about the subject matter of Mr. Masani's book. In commending it to the public I would only make one remark regarding it. It seems to me to stand out among all works that have been written about the Parsis and Zoroastrianism in this respect, that it tells the ordinary student in clear and simple form the things which he wishes to know. For the specialist there are the ancient texts and the scholarly works which have been written around them. For those who are not specialists, but who wish to know more regarding Parsi ways of life and thought, this is certainly the book.

JOHN McKENZIE

PREFACE

DURING the last few years I was often asked by publishing houses to write a book on the creed of Zoroaster.* I could not, however, make up my mind to essay the task, partly owing to other engagements and partly owing to diffidence concerning my capacity to do justice to the theme. At last, the necessary impulse came as the result of an invitation I received a few months ago from my esteemed friend the Rev. John McKenzie, then Vice-Chancellor of Bombay University, to give a short talk on the subject to a group of Christian students of religion.

At the gathering of that distinguished group of earnest seekers after truth I realized more vividly than ever before the keenness on the part of Christians generally to have some knowledge of the ancient religion which was preached, about three thousand years ago, to the vast population of a once mighty empire by the Sage of Iran, "the forerunner of those Wise Men of the East who came and bowed before the majesty of the new-born Light of the World," a religion which bade fair at one time to be the creed of almost the whole civilized world, and which, despite the loss of that empire and the vicissitudes of

* The name Zoroaster is the Greek form of the old Iranian *Zara-thushtra*, which will hereafter be used throughout in this work.

centuries, is faithfully followed to this day by a handful of descendants of the ancient Iranians. For these survivors, the modern Parsis, scattered all over the world, the voice of the Great Master is still a living voice. The echo of his clarion call to rally to the standard of the Spirit of Goodness and to rout the forces of the Spirit of Evil is heard till this day in their homes and places of worship.

Zarathushtra's outlook on life was one symbolic of the essential unity of the universe. In his system the entire creation forges its way towards the goal of perfection, and it is man's mission in this world to contribute towards the attainment of that goal. For the fulfilment of this glorious mission he must set his feet on the Path that leads mankind to the destined goal—the Path of *Asha*, or Righteousness. All other paths are no paths. Ahura Mazda, the All-Wise Lord, is the fountain-head of the Good Mind. The Good Mind is the basis of all good thought, from which originate all right-speaking and right-doing. On these three pillars, pure thought, pure words, and pure deeds, the Prophet of Iran reared the stately edifice of his ethical code, which influenced the life of the ancient Iranians for centuries and which is seen reflected, though dimly, in the conduct and character of their descendants. The creed of Zarathushtra may, therefore, be aptly described as the Religion of the Good Life; it is pre-eminently the religion in which good deeds are held up as the best and the most acceptable offering to God. Religious merit consists, according to the teaching of the Master, not in austerities, not in sacrifices and offerings to powers of evil, not in the cultivation of fugitive and cloistered virtue, but in the daily exercise of positive virtue and the diffusion of good deeds.

The pivotal problem of life is the problem of evil. On its solution hinges the destiny of mankind. The physical world, which man inhabits, is full of evil. There goes on within the heart of man a ceaseless conflict between the animal and the human, the diabolic and the divine. His life is, consequently, steeped in sorrow and suffering; yet it is a life worth living. The holy prophet, whose own life was an inspiring example of earnest ethical endeavour, calls upon his followers to accept the challenge of the principle of evil and to enlist themselves as comrades in arms with the Author of Goodness. This call to arms is accompanied by the cheering and inspiring message that if man but does his duty, good will prevail at last.

Not by mere negation of evil, not by retreat before it, but by facing it boldly and fighting it with all one's might may man hope to fulfil his lofty destiny to redeem the world from evil and to establish the kingdom of righteousness on this earth. He was but animal yesterday. He is man to-day. His destiny is to be angel, if not all at once, in the not distant hereafter, as the result of a gradual process of self-perfection.

The struggle within man's heart is merely a counterpart of the struggle which he encounters in the outer world. To eliminate disease and to make the world more habitable for his physical existence he has to fight and harness the elements. Similarly, he has to wage a crusade against the forces of ignorance, superstition, credulity, and bigotry for the emancipation of his reasoning faculty and for his intellectual progress. For his social advancement he has to combat social wrongs and social injustice, and for his moral ascent he has to wage the greatest crusade of all crusades, incessant war against his lower self.

The world is thus a battle-field and man the ally of the Beneficent Spirit in combating evil in all its manifestations. What is demanded of his followers by the Prophet of Iran is virile co-operation with the Spirit of Good in fighting the forces of evil. It is not enough that he should ignore or non-co-operate with evil. He should abhor it whole-heartedly and fight it vigorously. "Resist Evil" is the Zoroastrian battle-cry. In this essentially militant aspect the Zoroastrian concept of the good life differs from the ideals put forward by other seers who taught man to ignore evil or to meet it by passive suffering. They laid particular emphasis on the subjective realization of the good through a stoical suppression of desire and the attainment of perfect tranquillity of mind. Indifference to all causes of joy and sorrow and resignation to all evil and suffering are the natural corollary. Zarathushtra, on the contrary, stirs the hearts of his followers to positive hatred of evil, spurs them to join the crusade against the Spirit of Evil, and exhorts them not to evade the fight, or turn their

backs on the arch eneiny. .n his creed there is no
suggestion that the best defence against evil spirits
is to "direct towards them the strength of benevolence." Nor is there any suggestion for the propitiation of the powers of evil, or of any compromise
with them. Asceticism is unknown; renunciation,
monastic life, celibacy, mendicancy, fasts, and morti-
fication of the flesh have no place in his philosophy of
life. Penance, no doubt, is enjoined, but only as a
penalty for sins committed by thought, word, or deed.

Such is the moral groundwork of the Iranian
religion. Not merely to be good and to eschew evil,
but to do good and to resist evil, is its basic principle.
This is the supreme contribution of Zarathushtra to
religious thought and practice. His message of moral
duty and hope implies constant application of the
cardinal doctrines of the religion to the problems of
daily life. Constant endeavour to conquer evil builds
character; during the incessant struggle against the
forces of evil are developed traits of character such
as strenuous effort, industry, courage, justice, truthfulness, self-improvement, and self-sacrifice. To
cultivate these qualities is, therefore, a duty enjoined
by the Prophet on all his followers, and no religious
ideal or injunction could invest life with greater
dignity or help a man in getting nearer God more
than this battle-cry to resist evil and to fortify one's
self with an armour knit with those virtues which are
essential to secure the salvation not only of one's own
self, but of mankind generally.

Some of the sterling qualities of the Parsi community, which strike the other communities most, are its vitality, which has enabled it to withstand the vicissitudes of centuries; its adaptability to changing circumstances; its loyalty to the Crown; its industry and spirit of citizenship; and, above all, its philanthropy. To what extent these qualities are induced or stimulated by the religion which the community professes, is a question frequently asked. No attempt is made to answer this question in the following pages; the reader will be able to draw his or her own inferences from the bare statement of the fundamental principles of this religion and its code of ethics.

If conscience enjoins strict adherence to the principles and precepts embodied in one's prayers, if one lives, or even strives earnestly to live, up to those principles, one's conduct must necessarily be on a high level. The Parsis are a devotional people. Prayer forms the daily routine of their lives. Dr. Moulton vividly calls attention to this aspect of Zoroastrianism in the following words:

"And in a prayer for prosperity of all kinds to come on the worshipper's house, we read:

'In this house Obedience vanquish
Disobedience, Peace smite Unpeace,
Bounty vanquish niggard temper,
Piety impious rebellion,
Word true-spoken word false-spoken,
Asha smite the Druj for ever.'

"It is a comprehensive benediction; he who offers it has only to live up to it, and he will live thereby!"*

In presenting this book to the reader I lay no claim to originality or research. I have drawn freely on existing works on the subject, particularly on the splendid contributions made to the store of Zoroastrian lore by the late Sir Jivanji Modi, a name ever to be remembered in connection with Iranian studies with reverence and affection, and by Dr. Dastur M. N. Dhalla. The book is intended primarily as a handbook for non Zoroastrians. In Part I an attempt has been made to state and elucidate, as briefly as possible, the fundamental doctrines of the great religion, laying special emphasis on its ethical aspect. In Part II is given a brief account of Zoroastrian rites and ceremonies. This is mainly an abridgment of Jivanji Modi's excellent thesis on the subject, *The Religious Ceremonies and Customs of the Parsees*.

My grateful acknowledgments are due to all the scholars whose works I have consulted and whose authority is quoted at the proper places. I desire also to thank the Rev. Dr. John McKenzie for his valued foreword. What indeed could be more fitting than that one who incidentally suggested the composition of this thesis and who can speak with knowledge and authority, not only as a Christian minister, but also as a cultured scholar and public-spirited citizen, held in high esteem by the followers of all faiths in the cosmopolitan city of Bombay, should introduce this

* J. H. Moulton: *The Treasure of the Magi.*

book to the general reader? My thanks are also due to my kind friends, Messrs. B. N. Dhabbar, M.A., and B. T. Anklesaria, M.A., for going through the manuscript and favouring me with helpful criticisms and suggestions.

R. P. M.

BOMBAY

CONTENTS

Part One

PART ONE

PART ONE

Chapter I

THE BACKGROUND OF THE CREED

"The holy faith which is of all things best."

These are the simple words in which the Zoro-astrian creed is spoken of in the *Ushtavaiti Gatha*. The *Vendidad* is more effusive in its exaltation of the faith:

"As much as a great stream flows swifter than a slender rivulet, so much above all other utterances in greatness, goodness, and fairness is this law, this *daeva* (demon)-destroying law of Zarathushtra.

"As high as the great tree stands above the small plants it over-shadows, so high above all other utterances in greatness, goodness, and fairness is this law, this *daeva*-destroying law of Zarathushtra.

"As high as heaven is above the earth that it compasses around, so high above all other utterances is this law, this *daeva*-destroying law of Mazda."

Since the days of the *Gathas* and the *Vendidad* many a new religion has been embraced by different members of the human family, and none would venture to-day to indulge, while speaking of the creed of Zarathushtra, in the superlatives used in the Zoro-astrian scriptures. Nevertheless, a follower of the

Prophet may feel justly proud that the faith he professes once illumined the entire trans-Himalayan world, swayed the thoughts and influenced the philosophy of cultured Greeks and Romans, influenced also Judaism, and, through Judaism, Christianity, and Islam, and left its impress on the spiritual and intellectual development of the human race. In the sixth century B.C. Europe came to know of the religion and philosophy of Iran through Hostanes, the Archimagus who accompanied Xerxes in his expedition against Greece. In the fourth century B.C. Plato, Aristotle, and Theopompus show a knowledge of the work of the Magian prophet. In the third century B.C. Hermippus speaks expressly of these works as containing not less than 120,000 verses; and during the beginning of the Christian era Nicolaus of Damascus, Strabo, Pausanius, Pliny, and Dio Chrysostom mention, under different names, works attributed to Zarathushtra. In the third century St. Clement of Alexandria shows familiarity with the Zoroastrian scriptures, and later, the Gnostics make use of the Oriental cosmogony and psychology as derived from Zarathushtra. In the fourth century, according to the testimony of Eusebius, there existed a collection of sacred works of the Iranians. Empress Eudokia in the fifth century refers to several books of the Prophet, four of which treat of nature, one of precious stones, and five of astrology and prognostics."*

* Vide *The Dabistan or School of Manners,* by Mohsan Fani, translated from the original Persian by Anthony Troyer and David Shea.

Relationship between Zoroastrianism and Judaism

At one time Christian divines thought that the creed of the Sage of Iran was borrowed from the Jewish faith. In his classic work on the Connection of the Old and New Testaments, Dean Prideaux, misled by misguided authorities, went so far as to suggest that it was a copy of Judaism, and that the Prophet's familiarity with all the sacred writings of the Old Testament that were then extant made it "most likely that he was as to his origin a Jew!"* The theory has since been repudiated by many a savant, but as such misconceptions die hard, it is necessary to state at length, even at the risk of being prolix, a few historic facts and the inferences drawn therefrom by Christian scholars.

About six hundred years before the Christian era the Jews, who were carried away as captives to Babylon, were in constant contact with the Iranians. During the seventy years of their exile they borrowed from the Zoroastrian faith various doctrines such as the belief in the immortality of the soul, the resurrection of the body and future reward and punishment. "It is well known," says Max Müller, "that these doctrines were entirely, or almost entirely, absent from the oldest phase of religion among the Jews."† Dr. West elaborates this argument. "Few

* *Old and New Testaments connected with the history of the Jews and neighbouring nations*, Bk. IV, ii.
† Vide *Theosophy or Psychological Religion*.

Christians will be disposed to admit," he says, "that they owe their ideas of the resurrection and the future world to the traditions of the Mazdayasnian religion; and yet they will find it difficult to disprove it. Let those who doubt this fact ascertain how many decided references to the resurrection and future life they can find in the earlier scriptures of the Jews, written before they came in contact with the Assyrians and Persians, and then compare them with the more frequent references to the same subjects in the later Psalms and Prophets the book of Job, and the New Testament, all written after the Jews had become acquainted with Persian traditions. In fact, the book of Job has some appearance of being a translation, or adaptation from a Persian, or Assyrian text."*

In a luminous article contributed to the *Nineteenth Century*† on "Zoroaster and the Bible," Dr. L. H. Mills draws attention to what he calls "the now undoubted and long since suspected fact" that "it pleased the Divine Power to reveal some of the most important articles of our Catholic creed first to the Zoroastrians, and through their literature to the Jews and ourselves. . . . To sum up, I would say, as speaking from an orthodox point of view, that while the scriptures of the Old and New Testaments are unrivalled in their majesty and fervour, constituting perhaps the most impressive objects of their kind known to the human mind, and fully entitled to be described as 'inspired,' yet

---

* Introduction to *Mainyo-i-Khard*, 1871.
† January 1894; subsequently printed in book form.

the humbler but to a certain extent prior religion of
the Mazda worshippers was useful in giving point and
body to many loose conceptions among the Jewish
religious teachers, and introducing many ideas which
were entirely new, while as to the doctrines of
Immortality and Resurrection, the most important
of all, it positively determined belief. But the greatest
and by far the noblest service which it rendered was
the propagation of the doctrine that 'virtue is chiefly
its own reward,' even in the great religious reckoning,
and 'vice its own punishment.'''

Dr. T. K. Cheyne goes into greater details and
observes in his lectures on the Origin and Religious
Contents of the Psalter in the Light of Old Testament
Criticism and the History of Religions: "For centuries before the period of the Psalter, Iranian religion
had its own independent development, and its
doctrine of the 'last things,' as you will probably
agree, is peculiarly its own. A knowledge of this
first religion is necessary to the full equipment of an
Old Testament scholar . . . it is no longer ex-
cusable to study the Old Testament religion without
comparing Zoroastrianism." Later, he says: "Admit
a Zoroastrian influence upon Essenism, and all
becomes clear. The *fravashis* voluntarily assumed
mortal bodies in order to fight for God and for goodness against the power of the Evil One. Similar to
this, we may reasonably hold, was the belief of the
Essenes respecting the 'descent' of souls—a belief,
dependent for its full development upon Zoro-

astriartism, but not without Jew.sh germs. . . .
And what about the final act which I have ventured
to pos ulate for the Essenian drama of the soul? Is
that not also a piece of Hebraizca Zoroastrianism?
. . . The doctrine of an eternal life opened to all
the righteous, and involving a transfiguratior of the
body, is neither a mere evolution out of the old
Semitic belief in Sheól, nor yet a direct importation
from any foreign system of thougnt. Had it not come
into contact with Zoroastrianism, Israel would,
historically speaking, have struggled in vain to satisfy
its greatest religious aspirations. And yet it is not to
Persia alone that the Church-nation was indebted for
its greatest religious acquisition. . . . The distinction between spirit and body must have begun to
grow up long before this (the 73rd Psalm) that the
Jewish religion might be prepared for the moulding
influence of a more advanced system of thought. . . .
And what was this more highly developed system?
Zoroastrianism, if the preceding arguments are well-
founded.*

The Jewish Angelology and Demonology are also
based on Zoroastrian ideas concerning the *Amesua
Spentas*, or the Divine attributes personified as Divine
Intelligences; and the conception of the Evil Spirit,
which passed from the Jewish to the Christian religion, was also influenced by the belief in the existence of *Angra Mainyu*. Asmodeus, who figures in the
apochryphal book of Tobit, is positively the Mazdean

* *The Origin of the Psalter*, p. 394 and pp. 419–23.

wrath-demon,* *Aeshma Daev*. "This shows," says
Everett, "that a way was open, by which the Parsee
devils could enter into Judea; and if one member of
the evil host found his way thither, there is no reason
to think that he came alone. . . . Satan makes his
first appearance in Jewish literature in the Book of
Job. It is now claimed by the best authorities, such
as Davidson, Driver and Cheyne, that this Book was
written during the time of the captivity. It would
thus not be impossible that the writer should have
been influenced by Mazdean thought."†

The latest refutation of the theory of indebtedness
of Zoroastrianism to the Jewish faith comes from the
pen of one of the greatest modern students of religion,
Dr. Charles Gore. While dismissing the suggestion
of an alien source, he observes: "Clearly it is not
possible to suggest that this lofty religion—however
closely resembling the Jewish faith—could have been
borrowed from the Jewish: its date renders that
impossible. . . . Nor is there any other alien source
to which it can be attributed. It remains in its lofty
severity a momentous creation, if it be not wiser
to call it, as Zoroaster himself would have called it,
a signal inspiration by the divine Spirit of an individual prophet."‡

---

* What is here mentioned as a demon is mere personification of wrath.
† Article on the Devil in the *New World*, March 1895.
‡ *The Philosophy of the Good Life*, pp. 48–9.

Indo-Iranian Concepts

When one thinks of a religion, the questions which come uppermost to one's mind are: Who was its founder? Where and when did he reveal his faith? What was the state of society in those days? What was the background on which his creed rested? In attempting to answer these questions with reference to the religion of the Prophet of Iran, we find ourselves lost in the mists of time.

In the dim old days the Aryan ancestors of the present-day Parsis and Hindus lived together for long ages in a region which we have no means of locating definitely. When they thus kept together as one race and spoke the same language, the religion of the land was the religion of the race. The fiend of discord, however, caused a rift in the lute. Owing to a change of thought among the members of that happy family there was a cleavage. One of the sections migrated to Iran and the other to India.

According to the Avesta the *Aryas* ("the noble ones") had their original home in the fair land of *Airyana-Vaeja* (the cradle-land of the Aryas). Bal Gangadhar Tilak locates it in the Arctic regions whence the Aryans descended into the Pamirs.* It was far to the North where "the year seemed as a day." Both these branches of the Aryan stock divided the Universe into seven regions.

* *The Arctic Home.*

Of the common worship and common legends of the two sister communities a few relics have been preserved in the Avestan texts. The parallels in the Avestan thought and the Vedic concepts are, indeed many, but the contrasts which led to the schism are also numerous.

"From Nature to Nature's God"

Man then lived with nature. Upon the physical forces around him he depended for food and shelter. To him those forces appeared to be pulsating with life. The sun, the moon, the stars and the cloud above, the earth, the springs, the rivers and the trees below, were, he believed, presided over by invisible intelligences. In return for the bounties they respectively conferred, these deified elements were entitled to man's adoration and homage, which took the form of prayers and offerings, including sacrifice of cattle and fowl.

The empire of the beneficent intelligences was not however, absolute. Stricken by natural calamities such as earthquakes and storms, and smitten by disease and pestilence, man soon found himself face to face with malevolent agencies that appeared to contest the authority and thwart the beneficent work of the powers for good. The deification of natural powers was accompanied by the personification of man's own good and evil qualities. Virtue and vice appeared to have been fostered by some good or evil genius. Thus

man had as many ministering angels to adore as devils
to denounce and fiends to fight.

It was not so always. The traditional form of Aryan
belief, the belief, in fact, of the ancient Iranians and
the people of all the other branches of the Aryan
stock, was "from nature to nature's God." The idea
underlying this belief was that of an omnipresent,
omniscient, and omnipotent Creator of the Universe.
The religion in Iran long before the advent of Zarathushtra was *Mazdayasni*, i.e., the religion inculcating
a belief in and enjoining the worship of Mazda, or
the one all-wise God. Out of the nature religion grew,
as the result of man's thought, a sense that under-
neath the many there was the One and only One.
"From nature to nature's God" was thus but a
logical step in the evolution of religious ideas. At
times, however, this fundamental principle of the
essentially monotheistic creed was lost sight of and
people's reverence for the great powers of nature
degenerated into nature-worship and the adoration
and propitiation of gods many and lords many.

The Advent of Zarathushtra

Whenever the ancient belief was corrupted in this
way, prophets, or reformers, who are called *Saoshyants*
(benefactors of the community) came forward to
restore the religion to its pristine purity. Among
such reformers are mentioned Gayomard, Hoshang,
Tehmuras, Jamshid, and Faridun. The religion of

these eras is spoken of in the Avesta literature as
that of *Paoiryo-Tkaeshas*, i.e. of the ancients, or the
first religious leaders. In the days of King Gushtasp
of the Kayanian dynasty, the supremacy of the
Mazdayasni religion, or Mazda-worship, appears to
have been seriously challenged by the *"daeva-yasni"*
creed, the worship of *daevas*, or powers of evil, some
of whom are recognized as the Vedic and pre-Vedic
Aryan gods. Of these godlings some presided over
natural objects, others over evil qualities. Another
prophet or reformer, therefore, appeared on the
scene; the creed which he preached has, despite
many reverses and mutations, survived to this day
with not a few of its distinctive features preserved
practically intact. This prophet was the holy Zarathushtra Spitama, the descendant of Spitama.

To fix the date or place of birth of Zarathushtra
one has to make one's way through dark regions of
myth and history. It was believed that this sage of
Iran was born in Rae, but Sir Jivanji Modi has pretty
conclusively proved that he was born in Amui, or
Amvi, in the district of Urumiah.* The date of birth
is, however, still a matter of surmise. The oldest
classical writers, such as Xanthus, Plato, Pliny, and
Plutarch, place him in eras varying from 6000 B.C.
to 1000 B.C. Some of the modern authors give dates
varying from 1200 B.C. to 800 B.C. These are, however, speculations resting almost entirely upon in-

* In his *Zoroastrian Studies* Professor Jackson accepts Dr. Modi's discoveries.

ferences of doubtful value. Ancient Pahalavi writers place him about 300 years before Alexander the Great, somewhere in the seventh century B.C.; and modern scholars, including Professor Jackson and Dr. West, are of opinion that references in tradition and history to various incidents in the life of the Prophet appear to confirm the date assigned to him by those writers. Be that as it may, we have to go back at least 2,600 years to trace the background of the Prophet's creed.

The old traditional Mazdayasnan religion of Iran had still a hold on the people; but it was deformed. It was Zarathushtra's mission to reform what was deformed. To him belongs the honour of having raised a vague nature-worship into a definite and sublime theism. While preaching a pure and ethical monotheism, he emphasized the moral side of nature as no other prophet had done before him. Presenting in lofty and inspiring terms the ideal of the good life for man, this completely independent thinker taught most fervently, although surrounded by evil, that the ultimate controlling will in the universe was simply good, and that therefore good would prevail at last if man only resisted evil, lived his life well, and did his duty as enjoined in "the good religion of the Mazdayasnians." Taking his stand on that ennobling belief, he appealed to all good men and true for their co-operation in furthering the purpose of the good God. The idea of the good life was thus developed, for the first time in the

Aryan World, on very distinct lines, in the teaching of the Iranian prophet. Thus, perhaps for the first time in human history, the holy messenger cheered his disciples with his message of hope, which later found expression in many a creed and of which the following immortal lines of Tennyson would appear to be almost a verbal rendering:

"Oh! yet we hope that somehow good
Will be the final goal of ill."

Chapter II

THE PROPHET

Birth and Family History

To the warrior clan of Spitama, closely connected with the royal family of ancient Iran, belonged a devout and learned man named Pourushaspa. He was united in marriage to Dughdhova, daughter of a nobleman of Iran. She, too, was renowned for piety and devotion. This noble couple had five sons born to them, of whom Zarathushtra was the third.

The significance of the name Zarathushtra has puzzled many a scholar. The Prophet's ancestral name was Spitama. Some have suggested that Zarathushtra meant "possessor of old or yellow coloured camels," others that it meant the "high priest." It was probably the appellation by which he was known after he had proclaimed his religion, and which has been rendered into English as "He of the Golden Light," just as Prince Siddhartha came to be as the Buddha (The Enlightened One) and Jesus as the Christ (the Anointed).*

As in the case of other prophets, so in the case of

* See *The Religion of Zarathushtra*, by Dr. Irach Taraporevala.

Spitama Zarathushtra, tradition attaches various
miracles to his life upon earth. It is said that even
while in the embryonic stage the child glowed with
such spiritual lustre that everything around Dughdhova
was radiant with light, which increased in brilliance
as the time for nativity drew nearer. Instead of
crying, this infant smiled at birth* and, according to
the scriptures, nature also smiled with him in
sympathy.

> In whose birth and in whose growth
> Rejoiced waters and plants;
> In whose birth and in whose growth
> Increased waters and plants;
> In whose birth and in whose growth
> Cried out "Hail!"
> All the creatures of the Holy One.
> "Hail! born for us is the priest.
> Spitama Zarathushtra!" †

On the other hand, the Evil Spirit was confounded:

> At whose birth and at whose growth
> Rushed away Angra Mainyu
> From this earth which is wide,
> Round, whose ends lie afar.
> Thus he howled, the evil-knowing

---

* This tradition is recorded by Pliny, who observes in his *Natural
History*: "Zoroaster was the only human being who ever laughed on the
same day on which he was born. We hear, too, that his brain pulsated so
strongly that it repelled the hand when laid upon it, as presage of his
wisdom."   † *Yasht* 13, 93, 94 (Dr. Dhalla's translation).

Angra Mainyu, the all-deadly,
"Not did all the angels together
Drive me out against my will,
But Zarathushtra alone
Overpowered me in spite of myself.

"He smites me with the Holy Word, a weapon like a stone as big as a house; he burns me with Best Righteousness, as if with molten metal; so does he make it that it were better if I quitted this earth;

He alone who forces me to quit,
Who is Spitama Zarathushtra."*

Communion with the Lord

It was a strange world in which Zarathushtra found himself placed. The times were out of joint. Superstition had displaced true knowledge and sorcery true faith; false gods had dethroned the true God; the kingdom of God was overrun by the emissaries of the devil.

Zarathushtra's heart flowed out in deep piety and love to his Heavenly Father. He longed to see Him in spirit, to converse with Him, to reach Him, to serve Him, and to restore His kingdom on earth. It was not, however, a mission for a man engaged in worldly pursuits. If Zarathushtra wished to be the messenger of God to humanity, he must approach Him for the

---

* *Yasht* 17, 19, 20 (Dr. Dhalla's translation).

revelation of the true word to him. At the age of fifteen, therefore he withdrew from the world, a world in which, according to one of the Nasks, there was "not one just man, not two, not three, not several," and spent several years in retirement, thirsting for the moment when he could see the Heavenly Father in his mind's eye and commune with Him.

Whither he wandered and what he suffered and endured neither history nor legendary lore reveals completely. All that we are privileged to know is that he spent years in solitude amidst dreary wastes. There he stood alone, in the thick of the wilderness, alone with Nature, alone with his own thoughts and the reality of things; meditating deeply, while humanity was slumbering, on the eternal riddle of the universe, the great mystery of existence. There, in the sanctuary of Nature, this solitary seeker after Truth lifted up his hands to heaven and prayed, imploring Ahura Mazda, who filled all space, to take him to Himself, to meet him for but one moment and to speak to him by the word of His mouth about the mystery of life.

"This I ask Thee, tell me truly, O Lord: Who was the first generator and father of Asha (Law)? Who determined the path of the sun and stars? Who (has ordained) that the moon shall wax and wane? All this, O Wise One, and yet more, I wish to know."

"This I ask Thee, tell me truly, O Lord: Who upheld the earth beneath and the heavens (above) from falling? Who (created) water and plants? Who yoked the two horses to the wind and clouds? Who, O Wise One, is the creator of Vohu Manah (Good Mind)?

"This I ask Thee, tell me truly, O Lord: Who created light and darkness? Who made sleep and waking? Who (created) morning, noon, and night, that remind a man of his duty?"

At last, when the longing to see Ahura Mazda and the thirst for the vision divine consumed every other desire, Vohu Manah, the embodiment of the good mind, appeared unto the Prophet in a vision and led his soul in holy trance into the presence of Ahura Mazda. "Come hither to me, Oh ye Best ones," he prayed, "hither, Oh Ahura Mazda, in thine own person and to the sight, Oh Right and Good Mind, and I may be heard beyond the limits of the people. Let the august duties be manifest to all of us and be clearly seen."

The fulfilment of this prayer is recorded in the following words: "And I recognized Thee as the Beneficent, O Wise Lord, when I saw Thee first at the creation of Life, that Thou wilt make the deeds and words to be recompensed—evil for the evil and good for the good—through Thy generosity at the last turning-point of the Creation."

Now is his mind illumined, his soul entranced and he feels more and more of Ahura Mazda within him and without. Thanks to this divine illumination, he now reads sermons in stones and books in the running brooks, and sees all nature pulsating with the message of hope, traced with the hand of Ahura Mazda on plants and trees, pebbles and sands, banks of rivers and summits of hills. Now, indeed, the truth dawns on him; now is the enigma of life solved, and the herald of Ahura Mazda is ready to deliver His message of hope to mankind. Joyfully he turns his step towards his father's house, to embark on his mission of preaching the profound truth vouchsafed to him by the Lord, determined to make any sacrifice, to surrender even his life, in the service of Ahura Mazda.

The appearance of so gifted a seer and saviour unnerves the Evil Spirit, Angra Mainyu. "Do not destroy my creatures, Oh Holy Zarathushtra," says he. "Renounce the good religion of the worship of Mazda and thou shalt gain such a boon as was gained by the son of Vadhaghna (Zohak), who eventually became the ruler of nations." This offer the Prophet indignantly rejects. "No, no!" he exclaims, "Never will I renounce the good religion of the worship of Mazda, even though my body and my soul should separate."

Struggle and Success

For ten long years, however, no one paid heed to the Prophet, not even his friends and kinsmen. Denounced as a heretic and a sorcerer, he wandered from place to place before he could make a single convert to his faith. Deserted by kinsmen, forsaken by friends, harassed by foes, and persecuted by the

emissaries of the Evil Spirit, he turns to his Heavenly
Friend, and asks:

> To what land shall I turn, whither shall I go,
> Forsaken by kinsmen and nobles, am I;
> Neither do my people like me,
> Nor do the wicked rulers of the land.
> How then, shall I please Thee, Mazda Ahura?
> This I know, Mazda, wherefore I fail,
> Few are my flocks, and few my followers.
> In grief I cry to thee, Ahura, behold it.
> Help me ever as friend unto friend,
> Show me through righteousness the riches of the
> Good Mind.*

At last, he found his first convert in his cousin
Maidhyomah, the St. John of Zoroastrianism. Still,
however, people would not hear him. It was hopeless
to approach them until and unless he succeeded in
catching the ear of the highest in the land. He, therefore, decided to travel eastwards and went to Bactria,
where ruled King Vishtaspa. To kiss the threshold of
the royal court was not, however, an easy matter,
even for one who had communed with the King of
Kings. Long, long did he wait patiently for the
coveted audience. At last, on one auspicious day, he
found himself ushered into the royal presence. The
king received him kindly and allowed him to pro-
pound his creed before the nobles and learned men
of his court. So impressed was he by the prophet's

* *Yasna* 46, 1, 2 (Dr. Dhalla's translation).

message that he publicly embraced his creed, thus becoming the Constantine of the new faith. This was the turning-point in the history of the religion. The king's conversion was followed by that of the queen and of the courtiers. After this it was smooth sailing for the great Teacher.

Once established, the new religion spread rapidly throughout Iran and other lands. It must not be supposed, however, that while he attacked and denounced the false beliefs, superstitions and evil customs in vogue, Zarathushtra was allowed to preach the new creed unmolested. His growing success spelt disaster for the wicked chiefs and hypocritical priests who preyed upon the ignorance and credulity of the people. They succeeded by slander and deception in having the Prophet imprisoned on a charge of sorcery. The prison had, however, no terror for him. Surely, he was not alone in prison! Ahura Mazda dwelt with him and, with Mazda within him, nothing could harm him, nothing depress him. Thus, in marked contrast with Gautama Buddha, who turned his back upon a world that had no attraction for him and induced his followers to take the same road of renunciation, Zarathushtra resolutely faced the grim struggle of life and cheerfully went to jail in defence of his faith. Ultimately, he stepped out from the dungeon cell to carry on his propaganda to rout his persecutors, called Kavis and Karapans in the Avestan texts.

For well-nigh fifty years this herald of a new era

in the spiritual history of the Iranian people laboured
hard to deliver the message of Ahura Mazda, and at
last succeeded in gathering around him an ever-
widening circle of devoted disciples and zealous
adherents. After his religion had been thus firmly
established, he passed away, at the age of seventy-
seven, meeting the death of a warrior, in self-defence,
while praying in a fire-temple. According to some
authorities, he died in defence of the fire-temple
which was attacked by an enemy—an end worthy of
the valiant defender of the Cause of Truth.

Chapter III

REPUDIATION OF THE FALSE GODS

ZARATHUSHTRA's teaching has come down to us in the hymns called *Gathas*, which form the oldest part of the Avestan scriptures. In these metrical chants is enshrined not only the essence of his creed but also the story of the spiritual crisis that came on him and of the travail of soul and body that he endured. It would appear from this life-history of the seer that before he embarked on his mission he appealed to Ahura for answers to questions regarding the riddle of the universe with which he had wrestled for years. He felt that the universe must be essentially rational and that man's mind was capable of comprehending the ways and purpose of the All-Wise Creator. Besides the queries put and answers received by the Prophet, various discourses and exhortations are embodied in the Gathas, meant for the enlightenment of audiences composed of learned men, who had gone to Bactria from different parts of the country to hear him preach. The burden of his speech invariably was to induce his countrymen to forsake the worship of the *daevas*, or evil powers, to bow only before Ahura Mazda, and to separate themselves entirely from the idolaters of the day.

Exemplary Tolerance

Sweet reasonableness is a striking feature of Zarathushtra's teaching. He sings before the people the praises of the Lord and the hymns of the Good Spirit and implores every man and woman to choose his or her creed. "Ye offspring of renowned ancestors, awaken to agree with us!" These are the words in which in the course of one of his addresses he appeals to the good sense and understanding of the audience.* Earnestly he asks his disciples not to take any dogma or doctrine on trust, not to yield a blind and unreasoning submission thereto, but to invoke the assistance of *Vohu Manah*, the well ordered, good, earnest, and sincere mind, and to accept or reject his teaching after calmly examining all the pros and cons.

"Hear with your ears the best (saying)," he says; "see with your mind the beliefs of your choice; every man or woman to think for his or her self!"

Referring to the attitude of this eminently tolerant prophet towards the religion of his tribal tradition, Dr. Gore correctly points out that the Prophet does not appear directly to have combated it except where it was associated with vice. He merely strove to make effectual the reformation he proposed to inaugurate by offering and deepening the better elements in the tradition which the inner light showed him to be alone the truth.†

* *Yasna* 30.
† See *The Philosophy of the Good Life*, Chapter ii, p. 37.

No doubt he persuaded people to accept his creed as the best, but there was no intolerance towards other faiths, so long as they did not teach polytheism. Far from denouncing those creeds the Zoroastrian scriptures describe them as "better" religions, compared to the Mazdayasna creed invariably mentioned as the best. Nowhere in those scriptures does one find any trace of fanatic opposition towards those who did not embrace the creed, or any suggestion that the good and the pious can be found only among the followers of the Zoroastrian faith. On the contrary, it is frankly admitted that even beyond the pale of Zoroastrianism, piety worthy of reverence does exist. The *Fravardin Yasht* mentions a long list of the pious and the virtuous of the same country as well as of other countries that existed before, and their spirits are invoked, with a view to their example being followed, in these words: "We call upon the spirits of the pious men and women, wherever born, of those who have followed in the past, of those who do in the present, and of those who shall, hereafter in the future, follow the good religion." Such robust reliance in the supremacy of the truth and on the soundness of the doctrines preached by Zarathushtra, and such tolerance in an age when might was right and when the Prophet, backed by the powerful King Vishtaspa, could have commanded all the might of the State in propagating his doctrines, is indeed the most remarkable proof of the sublimity of the creed and the magnanimity of its founder.

Confession of Faith

The natural corollary to the belief in one supreme God was the repudiation of the army of false gods (*daevas*) that had invaded the old faith. The dominating feature of the creed was, therefore, a virile protest against the sway of those gods. It was a complete break with the earlier religion of the Iranians with its pantheon of the *daevas* and sacrifices of animals. The articles of faith to which a Zoroastrian was asked to subscribe, proclaiming this end, are embodied in the twelfth *Ha* of the *Yasna*, of which the following is a free translation:

"I join in annihilating the worship of the *daevas*. I profess myself to be a believer in Mazda (the Omniscient) as taught by Zarathushtra. I am opposed to the belief in the *daevas*. I am a follower of the law of Ahura. All the universe I attribute to the wise and good Ahura Mazda, the pure, the majestic; for everything, including the earth and the starry firmament, is His. . . . I repudiate the rule over me of false gods, evil, mischievous, adroit in inflicting harm, the most disgusting, the most deceitful the most pernicious in all existence. I denounce sorcery and all other black art. With all the sincerity of my thoughts, words, deeds, and token, I denounce the domination of false gods, and of those believing in them. Thus has Ahura Mazda taught Zarathushtra in the several conferences that took place between them, and thus Zarathushtra has promised Ahura Mazda in the

course of those conversations to disown polytheism;
so have Vistasp, Farshaostra and Jamasp promised to
repudiate the sovereignty of false gods; and so do I
likewise."

Thus was every initiate expected to serve as a
soldier of light, fighting for good against the forces of
Darkness and Evil. Owing, however, to a confusion
of ideas and a misconception of the counteraction of
good and evil in the system of the speculative philosophy of the Bactrian sage, and owing mainly to the
want of correct texts, Zoroastrianism was, until
recently, often described by European writers as a
dualistic religion. Such a conception ignored the
rudiments of Avestan theology. The fault, however,
lay not so much with those writers as with the
Zoroastrians of the later era, who themselves lost
sight of the original teachings of their prophet, confounded his philosophy with his theology, and gave
rise to a belief in the existence of an evil spirit co-
equal with Ahura Mazda.

No human race has passed through such singular
vicissitudes of fortune as have the Parsis; none has
been subjected to such tragic deprivation of its
scriptural writings as this band of survivors of a once
mighty race; no bible has undergone such frightful
distortions, mutations, and mutilations as the Avesta.
Thanks, however, to the recent researches of European
and Zoroastrian scholars, it is now generally recognized that the theology of Spitama Zarathushtra was
based on pure monotheism and that his conception of

Ahura Mazda as the Supreme Being is perfectly identical with the notion of Elohim, or Jehovah, found in the books of the Old Testament. The mention of the personality of an evil Spirit is nothing but a purely metaphorical statement of a profound truth concerning the existence of evil. Were it taken to signify dualism, scarcely any religion would escape the charge. If a belief in Ahriman, as the author of evil, makes the Parsi religion a dualism, says Dr. West, "it is difficult to understand why a belief in the devil, as the author of evil, does not make Christianity also a dualism."*

* Introduction to *Pahlavi Texts*.

Chapter IV

AHURA MAZDA

"Ahura Mazda, by Thy spirit, which is ever the same!"

With these words the Almighty Spirit is greeted in the Gathas as the Lord of Creation, the one Supreme Being, immune from all change through eternity.* From the ancient religion Zarathushtra took the name of *Mazda* for *God*, and to that name he prefixed the adjective *Ahura*, making the combined form *Ahura Mazda*, the All-Wise Lord, the Great Creator-Governor of the Universe. The entire universe is governed by God; hence He is called *Ahura*. Whatever is there in creation, whatever happens, is created or dispensed by Him; hence He is also called Mazda, Wisdom Consummate. *Ahura Mazda* is closely associated with the powers of nature, but there is no suggestion of pantheism in it. The Lord of Creation and the Universe are quite distinct. Ahura Mazda is above human as well as natural forces—creating, directing, and controlling them.

* *Yasna* 31, 7.

The Originator and the Embodiment of the Right Law

Asha, or the law of Truth, or the moral Law, appears to be often used as one of the names of the Supreme Godhead. In the non-Gathic Avesta *Asha Vahishta* is mentioned as one of the names of Ahura Mazda. In the following passage in the Yasna the Creator is addressed as *Asha Mazda Ahura*: "Those doctrines which I shall practise, and these actions which are contained in those doctrines, and those things which in the eye associated with Reason are worth the luminaries, and the suns, and the daylight increasing dawn—all these things will be for your homage, O *Asha* Mazda-Ahura!"

Thus the one Supreme Being, the Lord Omniscient, the Creator-Governor of the Universe, is represented as Himself an embodiment of the Right Law. The following passage renders the idea clearer:

"We shall not, O Ahura Mazda! displease you and Asha (the Law) and Vahista Mananh (the Best Reason) who have been endeavouring in the gift of praises unto you."

"When I first conceived of Thee, O Mazda, in my mind," says Zarathushtra in the well-known stanza in the Gathas in which he addresses God as Mazda and describes Him in His different capacities, "I sincerely regarded Thee as the First Actor in the universe, as the Father of Reason (Good Mind), as the true Originator of the Right Law (Righteousness), as the Governor over the actions of mankind."

Immune from Limitations of Time and Space

It will be seen that God in this aspect was not viewed as an abstraction. The Gathas present Him as the Living Active Existence, the Eternal Being, who can be perceived only in thought, but whose governance of the Universe is apparent to all, and who is ever to be served and adored. He is the Good Artificer, or Worker, through whom everything comes into life and exists. Brighter than the brightest of creation, older than the oldest in the universe, He sits at the apex among the Celestial Beings in the Highest Heaven. He knows no elder and has no equal. He is the first and the foremost. Immune from the limitations of Time and Space, He is Ever-the-Same, the most perfect Being; moving all, yet moved by none. The Greatest of all, it is He who has destined the benefits of His kingdom for all who lead a life of Reason and Truth. It is He who decides Victory between the rival hosts of good and evil. Everything comes from Him and through Him, the Lord of all.

This conception of Ahura Mazda, in the sense of the All-Being on the manifested plane of being, the creator, ruler, and preserver of the universe, without form, invisible, omnipotent, omnipresent, and omniscient, without beginning or end, who in Unity is all and is above all, is in some respects analogous to the idea of the Logos of St. John. He is the first born out of the Boundless Time (Zrvana), but not limited by time and he has existed from eternity in Boundless Time. Says the Prophet in the Gathas:

"O Ahura! I acknowledge Thee to be the Holy One when I first saw Thee at the creation of life, when Thou didst assign to works and also to words, their rewards—evil to the evil and good reward to the good—through Thy power, at the final end of the world."

"This I ask Thee, tell me truly, O Ahura! whether at the beginning of the Best Existence, the rewards will bring blessedness to him who wishes to have them. He, the holy (prophet), watches the transgression of all through his Spirit and is a life-healing friend."

"This I ask Thee, tell me truly, O Ahura! Whether what I shall proclaim is verily the truth. Will Asha (Righteousness) and its works render help (at the last)? Dost Thou assign power through Vohu Manah? For whom hast Thou made this earth the producer of joy?

"This I ask Thee, tell me truly, O Ahura! This religion which is the best of existing things, and which can prosper all that is mine in union with Asha—will they rightly observe this religion of my creed through the words and deeds of Armaiti (Piety) in desire for Thy good things, O Mazda?"

"This I ask Thee, tell me truly, O Ahura! whether I can put the Druj (Lie) into the hands of Asha and cast her down by the words of Thy lore, and work a mighty destruction among the wicked and bring torments and affliction upon them, O Mazda!"

"I will speak forth; hear and hearken, now, ye from near and ye from afar, that desire instruction. Now observe Him in your mind, for He is made manifest. Never shall the false teacher, i.e. the wicked one, destroy the life for a second time by leading astray men, with his bad faith and tongue."

"I will tell you what is best in this life. Mazda knows through Asha all things which He has created. He is the Father of Vohu Manah (the Good Mind). Aramaiti, through good deeds, is His daughter. Not to be deceived is the all-seeing Ahura" (xlv. 4).

"I will speak of that which the Holiest declared to me as the work that is best for man to obey. Mazda Ahura said: 'Those who at my bidding render him (Zarathushtra) obedience shall all attain unto Welfare and Immortality by the actions of the Good Spirit.'" (xlv. 5).

"I will speak of Him that is the Greatest of all, and I praise Him, through Asha, and who is bounteous to all that live. By the holy spirit, let Mazda Ahura hearken, in whose praise I have been instructed by Vohu Manah—By His Wisdom, let Him teach me what is best" (xlv. 6).

Nothing gross or immoral is connected with the character, or worship, of the Supreme Being. Therein lies the excellence of this system of theology. Evil in any form is abhorrent to God. No evil, positive or negative, ruffles His pure nature, for He is Goodness itself.

Different Names of Ahura Mazda

In the *Hormazd Yasht*, specially composed in praise of Ahura Mazda, we find a declaration concerning the different names of the Creator recorded in His own words:

"Reveal thou unto me," says Zarathushtra, "that name of thine that is the greatest, best, fairest, most effective, most *daeva*-smiting, best healing, that which destroyeth best the malice of *daevas* and men. . . ."

"God (Ahura-Mazda) replied unto him:

'My first name is, "I am," Oh holy Zarathushtra,
My second name is the Giver of Herds.
My third name is the Strong One.
My fourth name is Perfect Holiness.
My fifth name is the All-Good created by Mazda, the offspring of the holy principle.
My sixth name is Understanding.
My seventh name is He that Possesseth Understanding.
My eighth name is Knowledge.
My ninth name is He that Possesseth Knowledge.
My tenth name is Blessing.
My eleventh name is He that Causeth Blessing.
My twelfth name is Ahura (The All-wise).
My thirteenth name is the Most Beneficent.
My fourteenth name is He in whom there is no harm.
My fifteenth name is the Unconquerable.

My sixteenth name is He that maketh the true
account.

My seventeenth name is the All-seeing.

My eighteenth name is the Healing.

My nineteenth name is the Creator.

My twentieth name is Mazda (Omniscient).' ''

In some of the Pahalavï Pazand books we come
across such titles as Supreme, Omniscient, Omipotent,
Omni-Sovereign, Supreme God, and All in All. Dr.
Modi has made out a list of seventy-four names
indicating His attributes and powers as the omnipotent, omnipresent, and omniscient Lord of the
Universe.*

A peculiar panegyric in the Dinkard is also worth
recording:

"Sovereign and not subject; father and not progeny;
by himself and not descended from; master and not
servant; chief and not under a chief; possessor and
not indigent; protector and not protected; firm and
immaculate; possessing in himself living knowledge
and not through any medium; disposing and not
disposed; distributing but not receiving anything;
giving ease to others and not receiving it from them;
giving co-operation but not receiving co-operation;
esteeming and above estimation from others; directing
and not directed."

Each name of the Creator is a spell in itself. Whoever takes it on his lips and is engaged in meditation

* Vide *Moral Extracts from Zoroastrian Books*, p. 6.

of His attributes equips himself with the best of
armours to protect himself against the inroads of evil.
Even the Prophet himself is asked by Ahura Mazda to
repeat His names:

> "If thou wilt, O Zarathushtra,
> Vanquish all that hate malignant,
> Hate of demons, hate of mortals,
> Hate of sorcerers, hate of witches,
> Of the Faith's perverse oppressors,
> Two-foot heretics and liars,
> Four-foot wolves, wide-fronted armies
> Bearing on the bloodstained banner,
> Then these Names repeat bemuttering,
> All the day and all the night time."*

* *Yasht* 1 (Moulton's rendering).

Chapter V

COSMOLOGY

The Seven Keshvars

In the Avesta the earth is spoken of either as threefold or sevenfold. The division into seven zones (*Keshvars*) marked merely a progression of the original tripartite division. The intermediate Keshvar, *khaniratha*, co-incided, more or less, with the intermediate zone of the original division, and it was reputed to be the home of the ancient Iranians. The Northern and the Southern zones were each separated into two halves; and the Keshvar in the East and that in the West were new additions. In the Avesta the expression "the seven Keshvars" is used to convey the idea of the whole earth.

Order of Creation

The stars, the sun, the moon, the sea, all things high and low in the universe are unquestionably Ahura Mazda's own creation and they function in consonance with His own laws, but the crowning act of His creation is man. "Oh, Spitama Zara-thushtra," says Ahura Mazda, "I created the stars, the moon, the sun, and red-burning fires, the dogs, the birds, and the five kinds of animals; but better and greater than all, created I the righteous man.''

It was the desire of Ahura Mazda that His might, wisdom, and goodness should be utilized in promoting the happiness and enjoyment of mankind in this world. To enable man to play a meritorious part in the existence in the world below, and thus to equip him to soar higher and enjoy an exalted life in the next world, Ahura Mazda commenced the work of creation. It was from that moment that the present cycle commenced.

According to the later Avesta, at first were created the spiritual or the invisible creations. After these followed the corporeal, or visible, creations, namely, the sky, the waters, the earth, the vegetable world, the animal world, and man, the last of all beings. What He first brought forth were atoms, the particles which He put into shape. Every phenomenon in the universe is traced to the Creator and the Father of All. How this is done may be illustrated by the question put by Zarathustra to the Ruler of the Universe and the answer received by him, as recorded in the *Vendidad*:

''Oh Thou Maker of the material world, Thou Holy One (Ahura Mazda), is it true that Thou seizest the waters from the sea, Vouru-Kasha, with the wind and the clouds? That Thou takest them down to the Dakhmas? That Thou takest them down to the unclean remains? That Thou takest them down to the

bones? And that then Thou makest them flow back
to the sea Puitika?

"God Ahura Mazda answered, 'It is even so as
thou has⁺ said, Oh righteous Zarathushtra! I seize the
waters from the sea Vouru-Kasha with the wind and
the clouds; I take them to corpses; I take them down
to the unclean remains; I make them flow back
unseen; I make them flow back to the sea, Puitika.' "

Chapter VI

THE SEVEN IMMORTALS

"We worship the good, strong, beneficent guardian-spirits of the righteous, immortal benefactors (Amesha-Spenta), the rulers with their watchful eyes, the high powerful, swift, living ones of everlasting truth, who are seven of one thought, who are seven of one word, who are seven of one deed, whose mind is the same, whose speech is the same, whose deeds are the same, and whose Master and Ruler is the same, the Creator, Ahura Mazda." (Fravardin Yasht, xxii. 82–3.)

A merely abstract conception of the Supreme Being does not satisfy the yearnings of the human heart; it needs something tangible to which it can attach itself. Prophets and preachers, therefore, resorted to personification or deification of abstract ideas and attributes. The deities thus conceived ultimately came to receive better recognition than the Supreme Being. Thus, in India, although the Vedas emphasized the Ancient Truth and the One Truth, the people as a whole embraced or adhered to the worship of the Shining Ones, the gods whom their intellect could comprehend better than mere abstract aspects of the activities of the Godhead. Thus, also, in Iran, although

Zarathushtra assigned to no deity a position equal to
that of Ahura Mazda, six immortal benefactors came
to be worshipped along with Ahura Mazda as forming
a heptarchy of celestial beings.*

These six divine intelligences, as introduced by the
Prophet, are not so much angels as an integral part
of the Supreme Being, and they represent merely the
six outstanding Attributes of the Supreme Being.
Man cannot properly comprehend the Unity of God
without realizing the diversity within His unity; nor
can he understand His manifold activity without a
vivid realization of His attributes. To impress these
attributes effectively upon the masses, Zarathushtra
mentions them in the *Gathas* in direct association
with Ahura Mazda, the Wise Lord, as six divine
abstractions called the *Amesha-Spenta*, or the bountiful
immortals:

Vohu Manah	The Good Mind.
Asha Vahishta	The Best Order, or Righteousness.
Khshathra Vairya	The Absolute Power.
Aramaiti	High Thought, or Devotion.
Haurvatat	Perfection.
Ameretat	Immortality.

In course of time, these six attributes of Ahura
Mazda, to which was attached great sanctity, came to
be revered as beings next in rank to Ahura Mazda,
and in the later writings they are represented as being
all of one thought, one word, and one deed. Their

---

* Dhalla: *Zoroastrian Theology.*

father and lord is Ahura Mazda. The highest heaven
(*Garonmana*) is their dwelling-place. Their sanctified
names serve as the most mighty, most glorious, and
the most efficacious of the spells. To take any one
of these names on one's tongue is to acquire keys of
power.

These immortals are described as the shining ones,
of luminous eyes, exalted, mighty, valiant, imperishable, and righteous. They are the makers, modellers,
guardians, protectors, preservers, and rulers of the
creation of Mazda, and it is Mazda that has given them
beautiful forms. They hold their celestial councils on
the heights of the heavens. Thence they descend into
the seven zones into which, according to the Avesta,
the world is divided, and rule over the realms of the
earth. The faithful pray that the *Amesha-Spenta* may
visit their homes and accept their sacrifices. Radiant
is the path by which they come down to earth to
receive the libations offered in their honour. They
are the associates of the sun; and they gather together
the rays of the moon and shed their lustre upon the
earth. These spiritual beings also help in bringing
about the final restoration of the world, and each
one of them will smite his or her adversary at the
time of the Resurrection.

Zarathushtra invokes the Bountiful Immortals

Ahura Mazda asks His prophet to invoke the
Amesha-Spenta, even though he could not behold them

with his eyes. Obeying His behests, Zarathushtra
invokes them. He is the first human being to do so.
Following in his steps, the faithful pray to them for
help and protection. The ceremonies performed in
their honour by unholy priests have no delight for
them. Only the homage of the devout worshipper
reaches them. From such a worshipper all injury
and distress are warded off. When their votary
performs his devotion, he finds his spirit kindled
by the spark of their love. Forthwith he dedicates his
life to them and all that he possesses on this earth.

Vohu Manah

Seeing that this Universe was ruled by the First
Great Cause most wisely, Zarathushtra called Him,
as we have already noticed, by the proper name of
Ahura Mazda, the Wise Lord. Beholding that the
invisible and the visible world were pervaded by
His benevolence, he applied to this attribute the
name *Vohu Manah*, the Benevolent or the Good Mind.
Just as in Christian theology the Spirit is inseparable
from God, so is the Good Mind in Zoroastrian
theology. Again, just as in Christian theology the
Spirit is found in man, the divine within him, so in
Zoroastrian theology the Good Mind is found in
man, representing the genius of good thought, the
highest mental purity a human being is capable of
attaining. As the first in the creation of Ahura Mazda,
Vohu Manah occupies a seat in the Celestial Council

next to Ahura Mazda. His wisdom is classified into two distinct categories: innate wisdom and acquired wisdom. These two types of knowledge are worthy of propitiation and worship. Ahura Mazda asks the Prophet to seek knowledge throughout the night, because the true priest and his disciples work by day and by night to increase their knowledge. Vohu Manah is also the term used for Paradise; therefore, in the Zoroastrian scriptures we find the genius of good .thought welcoming the righteous souls to paradise. What, indeed, can be a more agreeable abode for the good man than the Good Mind? When the blessed ones cross the bridge and come up to the gates of heaven, Vohu Manah rises from his golden throne and greets them in gracious terms. In the final conflict between the hosts of the rival powers he will smite his adversary.

Asha Vahishta

Having noticed that the invisible and the visible worlds were subject to His Law or Order and Righteousness, the Prophet applied to this sublime characteristic of Order and Righteousness the name Asha Vahishta, the Best Order, or the Highest Righteousness. As the best order, the Law of the Universe is part of the essence of God; Asha is associated with purity, and purity is the core of the creed. *Ahura Mazda*, the Lord of Righteousness, has created *Asha Vahishta*, the greatest, the best, the fairest, the radiant, the all-good Beneficent Immortal. He is the smiter of disease, of death, devils, sorcerers and noxious creatures. There is but one Path, the path of *Asha*, that leads to eternal life; all other paths are false and misleading. Through *Asha Vahishta*, therefore, the devotee aspires to behold and be united with *Ahura Mazda*.

Good thoughts, good words, and good deeds make man *ashavan*, or righteous. He obtains purity only when he cleanses his self with them. There comes a day or night when the master leaves his cattle, or when the cattle leave their master and the soul leaves the body, but righteousness, which is the greatest and the best of all riches, accompanies the soul after death.

The adversary of *Asha* is Druj, deceit or wickedness. Asha is, therefore, invoked to enter the house of the faithful and to smite the wicked Druj. The faithful pray that a righteous king may rule over them, but that an unrighteous ruler may be confounded and overthrown.

We have so far spoken of *Asha* in its exalted sense of mental purity. There is still a higher sense in which *Asha* transcends both bodily and mental purity; in that deep spiritual sense *Asha* is equivalent to the Eternal Truth, or the Divine Law, in consonance with which God has fashioned the whole Universe, and which permeates the entire creation.

Khshathra Vairya

Both the invisible and visible worlds are governed by the absolute power of *Ahura Mazda*, which Zarathushtra designates *Khshathra Vairya*, i.e. the Absolute, or Sovereign Power. He represents the Perfect Strength, the Omnipotence, and the Universal Sovereignty of the Lord, and is invoked to help man along the path of Righteousness. The man who obeys the Law of God is blest with strength and power. In later times, *Khshathra Vairya* stood not so much for the supreme power or spiritual riches of the Divine Kingdom as for earthly wealth, and was hailed as the Lord of the Universal Kingdom, the Spirit presiding over mental and earthly riches. He was invoked as the helper and protector of the poor. Speaking of Khshathra Vairya as God's Kingdom, Moulton observes that the constant thought of the Kingdom of God as the supreme object of man's ambition is in the *Gathas* largely obscured by the difficult language, but that it is central and that there is no more significant link between the religion of the Iranian prophet and that of the Gospels.*

Armaiti

The invisible and the visible worlds exhibit in all directions the beneficent love of *Ahura Mazda*. Zarathushtra describes it as *Armaiti*, High Thought,

* *Early Zoroastrianism.*

or Devotion. It is devotion that sanctifies the heart and it is through the medium of devotion that the faithful aspire to traverse the Path in safety and approach *Ahura Mazda*.

"I choose for myself the excellent *Armaiti*; may she be with me!" The houselord prays that *Armaiti* may enter his house and rout heresy. She is the mother of Ashi Vanguhi, or the Spirit of Good Reward of Purity. At the time of death the pious Zoroastrian is left to the tender care of *Armaiti*. After the dead body is consigned to the Tower of Silence and the birds therein have commenced their work of destruction, all those who have assembled there offer obeisance unto Armaiti.

Later, *Armaiti* came to be identified with Mother Earth sustaining and nourishing all mankind upon her bosom. We have our birth from her; we are nourished by her and after death we rest in her bosom, until our earthly tenement is done with and mingled with the dust.

Haurvatat and Ameretat

As the First Cause pervaded the infinite space, and always existed and would always exist, Zarathushtra chose for these characteristics the appellations *Haurvatat*, Wholeness or Perfection, and *Ameretat*, Immortality, freedom from death, which invariably accompanies Perfection. These two *Amesha-Spenta* are closely united to each other and are always spoken of jointly in the *Gathas*. Together these two Bountiful Immortals symbolize perfection of health and immortality, which are the reward of the righteous after death; together they will smite the *daevas* of hunger and thirst during the final conflict between the forces of good and evil. On the physical plane they are respectively the guardian-spirits of the waters and of the vegetable kingdom, and their blessings bring perfect health and vitality of the body. Hence their connection with water and plants and their healing and health-giving properties. It is a truly inspiriting conception that these two attributes of the Creator, representing the salvation offered by Him in this world and the next, are always united. The seeker after eternal bliss has no need to undergo penance or austerities in this world. Immortality is not merely deathlessness; it is also the perfection of its accompanying blessing. It is, as Dr. Cheyne correctly puts it, complete happiness of body and soul, begun in this life and continued in an exalted degree in the next.*

All the *Amesha-Spenta* are thus symbolical of the attributes of the One Infinite and Eternal Being in whom is centred all existence, visible and invisible. In his conception of these attributes, Zarathushtra was unquestionably thoroughly original. They were the result of profound contemplation and the most distinguishing features of his creed. In later times, however, ignorance of the real significance of those

* *The Origin of the Psalter.*

highly abstract philosophical conceptions gave rise to the notion that these seven constituted a heptarchy of celestial beings, six of them being the holy immortals or archangels, with *Ahura Mazda* as their head. Zarathushtra's faith rested, as we have seen, in the belief in only one God, but after his death the monotheistic characteristic of his teaching was not maintained in its pristine purity and simplicity. Objects of nature, which he regarded as things created by Mazda and serving merely as symbols of God's greatness and might, gradually came to be regarded by his followers as objects themselves deserving of worship. Each manifestation of creation was believed to have been presided over by a special spirit, and thus a hierarchy of *Amesha-Spenta* and *Yazata*, i.e. good spirits, worthy of homage, was established, an idea wholly foreign to the doctrines preached by the Prophet. Researches of modern scholars have, however, thrown a flood of light on the fundamental and essential principles of the faith, which were for a while obscured by the accretions that had grown round them. "We need not hesitate," says Dr. Gore, whilst endorsing the conclusions reached, after prolonged discussions, by Moulton and other authorities, "to think of these holy beings as in the religion of Zarathushtra no more than personified attributes of Mazda and of His activities among men."*

* *The Philosophy of the Good Life*, pp. 41–2.

Chapter VII

THE ADORABLE ONES

"We worship the spiritual Yazata who are the givers of the better (rewards) and are full of Asha" (Gah. ii. 6).

Next in rank to the *Amesha-Spenta* come the *Yazata* (literally, the Adorable Ones), the distinction being the same as between archangels and angels in Christian theology. The number of the *Yazata* is legion. Only about forty, however, are mentioned in the extant *Avestan* texts and the most prominent of these correspond to the twenty-four referred to by Plutarch.* The number usually given, including the Holy Immortals, is, however, thirty-three. Ahura Mazda is Himself a Yazata, the greatest and the best of them, just as He is the first in the heptarchy of the *Amesha-Spenta*.

Numerous are the boons that these beneficent ones confer on humanity. They gather together the light of the sun and shed it upon the earth. Men invoke them with votive offerings and in return they help the worshippers. Offerings of milk and *Haoma*, of the *Draonah* (a sort of bread made of wheat) and of meat, too, are dedicated to them. Some scholars

---

* *Isis and Osiris*, 47.

have, however, attempted to show that meat offerings
are repugnant to the spirit and the teachings of the
Prophet; in fact, blood offerings are gradually dis-
appearing from the present-day ceremonies.

Although these Yazata find an honoured place in
the Zoroastrian pantheon, only three of them are
mentioned in the *Gathas*, namely, Sraosha, Atar,
and Ashi.

Sraosha

The first of the Yazata is Sraosha, the guardian
spirit of humanity, who typifies obedience to the
Divine Law. Professor Jackson designates him priest-
divinity, as he acts as an embodiment of the divine
service. He is in fact obedient to the commandments
of God. The first to worship Ahura Mazda, he
officiates as a missionary to teach humanity to the
world and to preach willing submission to Mazda's
mandates. As the evangelist of the true faith, he
moves about, disseminating religious lore over the
whole material world. Zarathushtra longs to see this
viceregent of God on earth and prays that the spirit
of obedience may come unto himself and unto every
man whom Mazda wills.

The dwelling-place of Sraosha is supported by a
thousand pillars; it is self-lighted from within and
star-spangled from without. He drives in a heavenly
chariot, drawn by four white, shining horses that are
fleeter than the winds, fleeter than the rain, fleeter

than the winged birds, and fleeter than the well-
darted arrow. His weapons consist of the sacred
formula *Ahuna Vairya* and the other consecrated spells.
He is the strongest, the sturdiest, the swiftest, and
the most active and awe-inspiring of youths. Himself
unconquerable, he is the conqueror of all.

In the later Avesta, Sraosha is portrayed as a never-
sleeping, wideawake spirit, who with his club up-
lifted protects all the material world, from sunset to
sunrise, from the onslaughts of *Aeshma* (wrath), the
prime originator of disturbance and disorder, chaos
and anarchy, and against all the forces of wickedness.
Three times during the day and three times during
the night he descends on earth, to smite the evil
spirit, and returns victorious to the ethereal regions
of the Amesha-Spenta. All evil vanishes from the
house, clan, town, and country, wherein the righteous
man thinking good thoughts, speaking good words,
and doing good deeds, welcomes and gives votive
offerings to this ministering spirit.

Sraosha also acts as a co-assessor with Mithra and
Rashnu, the triad constituting a heavenly tribunal
for the judgment of the souls of the dead. The
Prophet invokes this guardian-spirit of humanity as
the greatest of the heavenly beings to appear at the
final Consummation of the world. All death ceremonies are closely associated with Sraosha. The
funeral service begins with an invocation to him and
ends on the same note. On the morning of the fourth
day after death, the soul of the deceased crosses over

the *Chinvat* Bridge into the next world. There before
the judgment seat it has to render an account of all
its actions, and at this trial before the august judges
Sraosha gives evidence of its deeds.

Ashi Vanguhi

Sraosha's sister, *Ashi Vanguhi*, Holy Blessing, or
Good Reward of Deeds, is a feminine counter-part of
Sraosha. On the ethical side, she personifies sanctity
and symbolizes spiritual riches, or the blessings of
heaven, which are the reward of those who obey the
Eternal Law and seek the kingdom of God and His
Righteousness. On the physical side, she stands for
plenty and represents earthly riches. She fills the
barns of men with grain and with cattle, their coffers
with gold, their fields with foliage, the chests of
chaste women with jewels and their wardrobes with
fine garments. As the genius of plenty she joins
Mithra, who increases pastures and fodder. She, the
exalted one, is well-shaped and of noble origin; she
rules at her will and is possessed of glory. She is the
protector, guardian, helper, and healer of the good,
and the smiter of the wicked. The devout pray for
her presence and bounty; she follows the generous
man who rejoices the poor by his liberal gifts and she
fills his house with flocks of cattle and horses. She is
grieved at the sight of unmarried women and she
refuses to accept libations offered by childless persons
and women of ill-fame. As the zealous guardian of the

sanctity of married life, she guards the chastity of women, and abhors the wife who is untrue to the nuptial tie.

Mithra

Among the other prominent Yazata the most noteworthy are Mithra, Atar, and Aredvi Sura Anahita. The last two are so closely identified with the forms of Zoroastrian worship that they will need separate treatment. Only a few more words may, therefore, be said in this chapter about Mithra, the Indo-Iranian divinity, who attained the most dominant position in the Zoroastrian theology of the Later Avestan period.

Closely associated as he was with the oldest common cult of Iran and India, Mithra gradually became one of the most popular and conspicuous of the Yazata. His greatness is celebrated in one of the longest litanies in which he is spoken of in terms usually applied to *Ahura Mazda*. Nay, even the Wise Lord is there represented as having adored Mithra. Of all the celestial beings that rule over this earth, Mithra is the strongest of the strong, the sturdiest of the sturdy, the most diligent and intelligent among the divinities, the most victorious and glorious. Ever afoot, he is the leader of hosts, of a thousand devices, keeping ten thousand spies, all-knowing, the undeceivable, watchful, valiant, lordly, and heroic. His is the most dominating personality in the hierarchy, listening to appeals, causing the waters to flow and the trees to grow, ruling over the district, full of devices, a creature of wisdom. The swiftest among the swift, most munificent among the munificent, most valiant among the valiant, chief among the chiefs of the assembly, increase-affording, fatness-inducing, flock-giving, kingdom-bestowing, son-granting, life-imparting, felicity according, and piety-infusing. Whether there shall be peace or war between nations depends on his dispensation. Mithra is also a soldier armed with sharp spears and deadly arrows; woe betide the man who offends him!

Mithra's Associates

Ahura Mazda is the first and foremost among the associates who work in unison with Mithra. In the scriptures Mithra and Ahura are often invoked together. Their union is pre-Zoroastrian and corresponds to the Vedic *Mithra Varuna*. Mithra is also jointly invoked with *Hvarekhshaeta*, the shining sun, as one of his chief functions is to work as the guardian of light. He presides over light, especially over the light radiating from the sun. As the harbinger of light and herald of the dawn, he precedes the rising sun on the summits of mountains. The great vault of heaven is, therefore, his garment. *Ahura Mazda* and the *Amesha-Spenta* have built up for him a dwelling on the mountain Alburz, where neither night nor darkness, neither cold wind nor hot wind, neither sickness nor death, can ever reach. From this Elysian abode Mithra surveys the whole universe at a glance. Nothing is hidden from his penetrating gaze. His light is the dispeller of darkness and of all the sin and evil associated with it.

Protector of Truth

On the moral side, Mithra protects truth and is associated with *Rashnu*, who is the chief genius of truth. Light is synonymous with truth, as darkness is with falsehood. To utter untruth is the most heinous sin. All human evil is collectively summed up in the Avesta as the Druj, or lie. Of all the vices, lying is detested the most. The liar brings death to his country. The faithful is therefore warned never to utter false-hood, for Mithra never forgives liars. He is the protector of the lord of the house, the lord of the clan, the lord of the town, the lord of the country, but only so long as they lie not unto him. If they commit that sin, the wrath of Mithra works havoc with house, clan, town, and country; and along with these their lords and masters also perish. The sin of deceiving Mithra is, besides, visited for years upon the kinsmen of the offender. This canon of holding a man's family and kinsmen liable for his guilt is a survival of the primitive pre-Zoroastrian code of ethics considered essential for securing group morality.

Sanctity of Contracts

Mithra also demands of man fidelity to his pledged word. As the presiding genius of right, he guards the sanctity of oaths. The word Mithra in the Avesta is, consequently, often used as a common noun, meaning "contract." Ahura Mazda asks Zarathushtra not to violate a contract, whether it be entered into with the righteous or with the wicked, for Mithra stands for the inviolability of the pledged word.

Mithra's Wrath and Bounty

The faithful devoutly invoke Mithra by his name with offerings and implore him to attend to the worship, to listen to the invocation, and to accept the offerings. He then comes at the appointed time for help to the righteous man and bestows upon him radiance and glory, soundness of body, flocks of cattle, chariots, offspring, and sovereignty. If disregarded in worship or angered, he inflicts poverty and misery upon the offender, depriving him of his offspring and power. To invoke him by his name is to obtain the key to happiness in this as well as in the next world.

Chapter VIII

THE CULT OF FIRE

OF the guardian spirits connected with the four elements, Atar (Fire) receives the exalted distinction of being *Puthro Ahurahe Mazdao*, "the son of *Ahura Mazda*." In the Vedas an analogous expression is used for lightning, which is spoken of as the "son of *Asura Varuna*." The principal terms expressing the Aryan idea of the divinity are borrowed from light and fire. The general name for God in Sanskrit is *Deva*, i.e. the shining, from the root *div*, to shine. Lightning is also called in the old Sanskrit *Atharvan*, i.e. having *Athar*, i.e. fire. This would show that the cult of fire was by no means a peculiar feature of the Iranian creed; it was common to other Aryan nations and had come down from remote antiquity. Like their Vedic brethren, the ancient Iranians spoke of the fire with its towering flames as a messenger from the earth to the high throne of *Ahura Mazda*, and they established Atar as a symbol of worship.

What, indeed, can be a more natural and more sublime representation of Him, who is Himself Eternal Light, than a pure, undefiled flame? Zarathushtra mentions Atar more in the sense of the divine spark,

a spark of the divine flame that glows in the heart of
every human being rather than as the holiest of the
elements venerated as the source of heat and light,
life and growth. He selected it as the outward symbol
of his faith because, being the holiest of the elements,
it symbolized the divine spark within. He restored not
only the unity of God, but also the most ancient
characteristic Aryan form of divine service, the worship of fire, as a symbol of God.

The Romans, who evidently separated from the
original Aryan stock at a much earlier date than the
Brahmans, had the ancient Flamines as fire-priests,
whose office it was to kindle the fire, literally, to
enflame or draw forth the flame. The fire of their
hearths could not be carried away except for sacred
purposes. They were not allowed to touch anything
unclean, neither a dead body nor a grave; nor to go
out without the *pileus*, a long-pointed, flame-like
head-cover, on the apex or point of which a *virga*,
or twig of an olive tree, and a *filum* were attached.
When going to sacrifice, they held in their hand the
virga commetacula, perhaps corresponding to the
Zoroastrian *baresam*. Their wives, *Flaminicae*, wore a
similar conical head-dress and the *flammeum* a yellow
or flame-coloured veil. So wholly did the Flamines
belong to the Divinity, that even the cuttings
of their hair and the parings of their nails had
to be buried under a fruit-bearing tree, which
recalls the exhortation to the Prophet of Iran in the
Vendidad:

"O Zarathushtra, cut the hair, trim the nails, and
carry them thither."

The Romans had also at Alba Longa the federal
altar, from which thirty Latin towns received their
sacred fire. The hearth of Vesta at the foot of the
Palatine Hill in Rome was the sacred centre for the
whole Roman State. The eternal fire on it symbolized
the presence of God and the protection of Heaven
and of the State's existence. So also among the Greeks
there was at Olympia an altar of *Pan* the fire on which
was never allowed to be extinguished. In the temple
of *Athere Polias* an ever-burning golden lamp was
kept. Xerxes spared the sanctuary of Delos, because
of the similarity of its fire-worship to that of the
Zoroastrian.

The old Germans had an ever-burning lamp placed
before the statue of their god Thor. The Slavs had in
honour of their god *Perun*, and the Prussians in
honour of their *Perkun*, an everlasting fire which the
sacrificing priest was obliged to maintain with oak-
wood. The Lithuanians had in Wilna an ever enduring
fire, *Zinoz*. Woe to the priests who permitted it to
go out! Death was the only punishment for such a
sin. The sacred flame in the temple of the Slavic
"God of Light" could not be approached by the
priests except whilst keeping back their breath; a
custom reminding us of the *padan*, the small piece
of cloth with which the Parsi priests cover their
mouths when serving the fire, so as to protect it from

being polluted by their breath. At Kildare, in Ireland, a perpetual fire, like that of the Roman Vesta, was maintained in hour of the pagan *Bridgit* "the Bright"; it was surrounded by a fence, which no man was allowed to approach, and was not to be blown with the mouth, but only with bellows.

The Jewish religion had its shining flames and burning fires as emblems of God's majesty and presence. "The fire on the altar," said the Lord, speaking to Moses, "shall always burn and the priest shall feed it, putting wood on it every day in the morning. This is the perpetual fire, which shall never go out on the altar." St. John the Baptist spoke of the Christ when he said to the Jews: "I indeed baptize you with water unto penance; but he who is to come after me is stronger than I, whose shoes I am not worthy to carry; he shall baptize you with the Holy Ghost and with fire." This was confirmed by Christ when he said: "I am come to send fire on the earth, and what will I, but that it be kindled?" Hence, when after his ascension, the Apostles were all united in a chamber at Jerusalem, suddenly, in imitation of the proclamation of the Old Law on Mount Sinai, "there came a sound from Heaven as of a mighty wind coming; and it filled the whole house where they were sitting. And there appeared to them cloven tongues as it were of fire; and it set upon each of them: and they were all filled with the Holy Ghost." In the sanctuary of the Christian Church the Sacred flame indicates the Sacramental presence of God, the

Redeemer, just as in the sanctuary of the Zoroastrian fire-temple the perpetual flame indicates the presence of *Ahura Mazda.*

In these fire-temples the Zoroastrians pay deep homage to Atar. Many a hymn has been composed in his praise. He is the most beautiful, the lord of the house, of renowned name, the beneficent crusader, full of glory and healing powers. The devout Zoroastrian who worships the fire with fuel in his hand, with the *baresman* twigs in his hand, with milk in his hand, with the mortar for crushing the branches of the sacred *Haoma* in his hand, is blest with happiness. Among the boons sought of this ministering *Yazata* are well-being and sustenance in abundance, comprehensive and imperishable wisdom, which stands for reverence, knowledge, holiness, a ready tongue, worthy children, name and fame in this world, and the bliss of paradise. Whoever does not pay due homage to the fire displeases *Ahura Mazda.*

In the *Atas* Nyahesh the devout Zoroastrian prays for the preservation of the fire in his house till the Day of Renovation: "Mayest thou burn in this house! Mayest thou ever burn in this house! Mayest thou blaze in this house! Mayest thou increase in this house, even for a long time, until the time of the good, powerful renovation of the world!"

When Mithra goes on his daily round in his golden chariot, Atar drives behind him along with the other intelligences. Together with Vohu Manah he smites

the Evil Spirit who has committed the sin of burning
or cooking dead matter. For those who commit this
sin the *Vendidad* enjoins capital punishment. There is
no purification for the man who carries a corpse to
the fire. A fire defiled by dead matter must be cere-
monially purified; to take to the altar the embers of a
fire so purified is a deed highly meritorious and
deserving of reward in the next world.

The Fire Temples

Such anxiety to prevent fire from being desecrated
and to prescribe an elaborate code for its purification
in case of defilement can best be appreciated if it is
borne in mind that, regarding fire as the highest
emblem of divinity and as the holiest symbol of their
faith, the devout followers of Zarathushtra have
installed it in their temples and offer it their worship
to *Ahura Mazda*. In these temples, known as Atas-
Behrams, the sacred flame is permanently kept
glowing by day and by night. To offer sandalwood to
the fire is regarded as an act of merit. No wonder
sandalwood worth thousands of rupees is used in
the fire-temples every year.

Misconception of the Cult

Later, the conception of the element itself was
confused with that of the spirit said to reside within

it. This confusion of ideas gave rise to misconceptions.
Fire occupies merely a subordinate, though important,
place in the religious system of Zarathushtra. In it
he merely recognized the type of Immortal Light and
the spiritual resurrection of the Soul. In the Gathas
he speaks of fire as a bright and powerful creation of
Ahura Mazda and prefers it, as a symbol of divinity,
to idols and other created objects. Nowhere does he
enjoin the worship of fire. Yet, in Europe as well as
in Asia, the idea prevailed for a long time that the
Zoroastrian religion consisted entirely of fire-worship.
This theory has long been exploded. Max Müller
disposed of it with the observation that if the religion
of Zarathushtra were called fire-worship, the same
name ...would have to be applied to the religion of
India, nay, even to the religion of the Jews. Indeed,
one has to view the attitude of the Zoroastrian community towards this sacred symbol side by side with
its adoration of other sacred elements. One might
as well regard Zoroastrians as sun-worshippers,
because they turn to it in reverence and lift their
hands in prayer before it, or water-worshippers,
because they recite their prayers before the waters
of wells, springs, and seas! If by "worship" of a
sacred element is implied reverence for it and glori-
fication of it, then the Zoroastrian praying before
the sacred fire for the blessing of longevity, strength,
wisdom, happiness, and virtuous progeny, unquestionably worships fire. Such veneration, however, does not
imply that the object adored is taken to be the

supreme Deity. Nor is such adoration inconsistent with a religious system based on monotheism, and it should leave little room for misunderstanding, especially in view of similar homage paid by the Zoroastrians to other sacred elements.

Chapter IX

THE PRESIDING GENIUS OF WATER

VENERATION of water, another phase of nature-worship, has come down to the followers of the faith of Zarathushtra from their Aryan ancestors. It must be remembered, however, that water-worship was imbibed rather than engendered by Aryan culture. From remote ages man endowed trees, plants, stocks, stones, dales, hills, seas, and springs with spirits visible and invisible. It was a stage in cultural progress through which he had to pass, the stage when he believed in myriads of spirits whose ubiquity has been aptly characterized as an unholy travesty of the Divine Omnipresence. It was upon such a spirit-world of pre-historic man that the primeval nature-worship of the Aryans was based. Water to them was not only the prime necessity of life, but the very birth-place of life, worthy of worship as divinity. In the *Vedas* waters are called *apo-devi*, and in the *Avesta*, *apo vangrhish*.

The *Gathas* of Zarathushtra, however, recognize no water deity. His purely monotheistic creed recognized only one creator of all the Universe, of all the elements: "O Ahura Mazda," he asks, "who but

Thee created waters and trees?" In the later *Avesta*, however, we find the development of a regular cult of water-worship with the deity *Aredvi Sura Anahita* as the presiding genius of water.

According to the conception of those times the abode of waters was in heaven and their descent from heaven was poetically pictured as the coming down of the fair maidens and daughters of "Ahura," the Lord, to the nether regions. The Avestan people greeted these beneficent divinities as Ahurani (Vedic Asurani), just as the Babylonians hailed their goddess of water as Mylitta, derived from *mul*, Arabic *maula*, the Lord.

Aredvi Sura Anahita

In the *Aban Yasht* the river is addressed as a mighty goddess, Aredvi Sura Anahita, strong, sublime, spotless, Aredvi Sura being the name of a mythical river. She dwells in the starry regions and Ahura Mazda has assigned to her the work of guarding the holy creation just as a shepherd guards his flock.

Ahura Mazda calls upon Zarathushtra to worship Anahita, who rolls under bridges, gives salubrity, defeats the *daevas*, professes the Ahurian religion, and who deserves praises and worship in this living world:

"The wide-expanding, the healing,
Foe to the *daevas*, of Ahura's Faith,
Worthy of adoration in the material world,
Worthy of prayer in the material world,

> Life-increasing, the righteous,
> Herd-increasing, the righteous,
> Food-increasing, the righteous,
> Wealth-increasing, the righteous,
> Country increasing, the righteous.

.   .   .   .

> Whom I, Ahura Mazda, by movement of tongue
> Brought forth for the furtherance of the house,
> For the furtherance of the village, town, and
>   country."

Aredvi Sura Anahita has a chariot of her own, drawn
by four great chargers, all of them white and of the
same stock, who defeat all tyrants, wicked men,
sorcerers, witches, oppressors, as well as those who
are wilfully blind and wilfully deaf. This is, of course,
an allegory. We are told that the four steeds are the
wind, the rain, the cloud, and the sleet, and that it
was Ahura Mazda who made them for her.

A vivid picture of this water-spirit is drawn in the
texts. She is a maiden, handsome in figure and appearance, well-shaped, pure, and having a halo around her.
Upon her head she wears a golden crown set with a
hundred stars and beautifully embellished; golden
ear-rings adorn her ears, a golden necklace decks
her neck, and elegant bracelets illumine her arms.
Around her waist she has a girdle which lends addi-
tional grace to her beautiful figure and she wears
golden shoes to match her garment of gold. This
word-picture of the spirit of the waters has been

described by some scholars as a faithful reproduction
of Anahita's statues in stone and metal. It must
not be supposed, however, that image-worship was
common in Iran. Idolatry in any form was repugnant
to orthodox Zoroastrianism; and Iranian kings and
heroes waged a crusade against idol-worship. Herodotus testifies that the people of Iran knew no idols.
During the Achaen.enian period, however, statues
of different divinities were not unknown, and
statues were erected in honour of Aredvi Sura
Anahita in Babylon, Ecbatana, S·sa, Persepolis,
Bactria, Damascus, and Sardis. Whether those statues
were worshipped by the Zoroastrians of the time along
with the other communities living with them, it is
not possible to state with any degree of accuracy.

The *Aban Yasht* recounts the names of the kings
who gave offerings to Aredvi Sura Anahita, and
begged for various favours. Even Ahura Mazda, it is
said, worshipped her in order to seek her assistance
in inducing Zarathushtra to become His prophet.
Zarathushtra invokes her with the Haoma and the
Baresman, with spell. and libations. Other votaries
offer her a hundred stallions, a thousand oxen, and
ten thousand sheep. Haoshaynha, Yima, Thraetaona,
Keresaspa, and a host of other monarchs, heroes,
sages, and celebrities, all adore her and ask for divers
boons. The rulers pray for sovereignty over countries,
the warriors for swift horses and victory on the battle-
field, the priests and their disciples for knowledge
and wisdom to answer the riddles propounded by

heretics, and the priest who offers libations implores her to descend from her celestial abode to the altar and to grant riches, horses, chariots, swords, food, and plenty to mankind. The wicked, however, could not hope to win her favours. Azi Dahaka (an incarnation of the Evil Spirit) implored her to endow him with the strength to slaughter all the men on the surface of the earth and to clear all the seven zones of the human race, but she refused to grant the prayer. Similarly, boons solicited by other national foes of Iran are refused.

Penalty for Defilement of Water

It is sinful to contaminate water. Such an act offends the presiding spirit of the waters. Those who knowingly take dead matter to the waters become unclean for ever. Should a man, while walking or running, riding or driving, happen to see a corpse floating in a river, he must go down into the river ankle-deep, knee-deep, waist deep, even full depth if need be, and remove the putrid body from the waters and place it upon dry ground exposed to the light of the sun.*

An Ideal Mode of Worship

The homage originally offered to the waters of the spring is extended by modern Zoroastrians to the

* For corresponding beliefs among other people see *Folklore of Wells*, by R. P. Masani.

waters of wells and seas. In Bombay city, the strong-
hold of this small band of Zoroastrians, any day along
the beach, and at almost any hour of the day, may be
seen devout Parsis dipping their fingers in the water,
applying it to their eyes and forehead and lifting up
their hands in prayers to Ahura Mazda. Andrew
Carnegie has left behind an interesting description
of such a sight witnessed by him at Bombay during a
voyage round the world. "This evening," he says,
"we were surprised to see, as we strolled along the
beach, more Parsees than ever before, and more
Parsee ladies, richly dressed, all wending their way
towards the sea. . . . Here on the shore of the
ocean, as the sun was sinking in the sea, and the
slender silver thread of the crescent moon was
faintly shining on the horizon, they congregated to
perform their religious rites. Fire was there in its
grandest form, the setting sun, and water in the vast
expanse of the Indian Ocean outstretched before
them. The earth was under their feet, and, wafted
across the sea, the air came laden with the perfumes
of 'Araby the Blest.' Surely, no time or place could
be more fitly chosen than this for lifting up the soul
to the realms beyond seas. I could not but participate
with these worshippers in what was so grandly
beautiful. There was no music save the solemn moan
of the waves as they broke into foam on the beach.
But where shall we find so mighty an organ, or so
grand an anthem? How inexpressibly sublime the
scene appeared to me and how insignificant and un-

worthy of the unknown seemed even our cathedrals 'made with human hands,' when compared with this looking up through nature unto nature's God! I stood and drank in the serene happiness which seemed to fill the air. I have seen many modes and forms of worship—some disgusting, others saddening, a few elevating when the organ pealed forth its tones, but all poor in comparison with this. Nor do I ever expect in all my life to witness a religious ceremony which will so powerfully affect me as that of the Parsees on the beach of Bombay."

Carnegie was but one of numerous visitors from the West who were thus captivated by this mode of worship. Samuel Laing sees in it an ideal opportunity to pay one's homage to the Good Spirit and to look into the abysses of the unknown with reverence and wonder. "Here is an ideal religious ceremony," he observes, "combining all that is most true, most touching, and most sublime, in the attitude of man towards the Great Unknown. Compare it with the routine of an ordinary English Sunday, and how poor and prosaic does the latter appear! And now, before I take my final leave of the reader, let me for a few moments throw the reins on the neck of fancy, and suppose myself standing with that group of Parsees by the shore of the Indian Ocean, listening to its murmured rhythm, inhaling the balmy air, watching the silver crescent of the new moon, and musing on the wise sayings of the ancient sage; the sum of the reflections which I have tried to embody in the preceding pages would take form and crystallize in the following sonnet:

"Hail! Gracious Ormuzd, author of all good,
Spirit of beauty, purity, and light,
Teach me like thee to hate dark deeds of night,
And battle ever with the hellish brood
Of Ahriman, dread prince of evil mood,
Father of lies, uncleanliness, envious spite,
Thefts, murders, sensual sins that shun the light,
Unreason, ugliness, and fancies lewd.
Grant me. bright Ormuzd, in thy ranks to stand,
A valiant soldier faithful to the end;
So when I leave this life's familiar strand,
Bound for the great Unknown, shall I command
My soul, if soul survive, into thy hand
Fearless of fate if thou thine aid will lend."*

Had those admirers of the Zoroastrian mode of worship been initiated into the esoteric meaning of the so-called worship of the elements, they might have appreciated all the more the Parsi's adoration of Fire and Water. The material fire and water which he makes his *Kebleh*, or altar of divine worship, are but the symbols of the spiritual Fire and Water which he holds in the mind's eye. It is not the elements of fire and water which he worships, it is the spirits residing in these material elements, the spiritual fire and water, named, respectively, "*Atarsh puthra Ahurahe Mazdao*," i.e. "Fire, son of Ahura

* *A Modern Zoroastrian.*

Mazda," and "*Aredvi Sura Anahita*," "the Righteous, shining, undefiled spirit of waters," that he adores. That fire is the Fire which is in *Garonmana*, shining before Ahura Mazda; and that spirit of the waters, *Aredvi Sura Anahita*, is in the same way the spiritual source of all the waters that flow on the face of the world.

Chapter X

THE PROBLEM OF GOOD AND EVIL

THE most bewildering problem of life is that of existence of evil. There is a bright as well as a dark side to creation; man, too, has his noble as well as his ignoble side. An inescapable dualism besets nature. All is not right with the Universe, nor is it all wrong. With much that is good in it, there is a good deal of evil, which cannot be ignored, or sophistically explained away as *maya*, or illusion. Nor can it be tolerated, in the spirit of a fatalist, as an inscrutable decree of Providence.

Evil is Positive

Zarathushtra postulates the independent existence of evil; it is just evil, nothing more nor less. It is not good sullied or corrupted, nor is it good in the process of formation or fructification; much less is it the mere negation of good. It is a distinct principle and the active enemy of good. Both these principles of good and evil are incessantly at work in man as well as in creation; and the story of their conflict is the story of the world. In this great conflict, man is a co-worker and a fellow-combatant on the side of *Spenta Mainyu*, the Beneficent Spirit. The Prophet of Iran induces in his followers a militant instinct, a fervent longing to combat the Evil Spirit. Life thus becomes an interminable crusade against the forces of evil and imperfection. Not only man, but the entire creation has to rise from the abyss of imperfection to the summit of perfection. During this process social wrongs have to be adjusted; social justice has to be rendered; society as a whole has to be regenerated; the world has to be redeemed.

The Two Primeval Principles

Having arrived at the basic idea of the unity of God, Zarathushtra found himself confronted by the problem of the eternal conflict going on in the world between good and evil since the dawn of creation. How could the imperfections found in the world, the various kinds of evil, injustice, and exploitation, wickedness and baseness, be compatible with the holiness, beneficence, and justice of Ahura Mazda? God-given life surrounded on all sides by evil and steeped in sorrow and suffering is, indeed, an anomaly. The Sage of Iran furnished a solution of this mystery by positing two primeval powers at war with each other. One of these Principles is called Spenta Mainyu, the Beneficent Spirit, and the other Angra Mainyu, the Evil Spirit. There is nothing in the Gathas to show that both the spirits emanated from or were the creation of Ahura

Mazda. Although some authors draw such an inference, the position may best be stated as put by Professor Jackson. The two Spirits do not exist independently, but each in relation to the other; they meet in the higher unity of Ahura Mazda. They existed before the beginning of the world, but their opposition only finds expression in the world that we see. The Beneficent Spirit is not entirely free to do as he pleases; ever since he came into being he has been encountering opposition from the Evil Spirit.

These twin Spirits form, indeed, the very antithesis of each other in every respect. How radically they differed from and opposed each other is declared in the Gathas in the following emphatic terms:

"Now shall I speak of the Spirit Twain at the first beginning of Life, of whom the Holier thus addressed the Evil one: 'Never shall our minds harmonize, nor our doctrines; neither our aspirations, nor yet our beliefs; neither our words, nor yet our deeds; neither our hearts, nor yet our souls.' "*

Thus for the first time in the history of religion we see the philosophic doctrine of Eternal Polarism propounded by the Prophet of Iran, a doctrine which, far from inducing a belief in cosmic dualism, served to reinforce the belief in uncompromising monotheism, which was the keynote of his creed. Our sublunary world is, so to speak, a battle-ground for the opposite forces of good and evil. Both the principles are constantly at work in man as well as in creation. It is man's

* Yasna 45, 22.

duty and highest mission on earth to rally to the banner
of the King of Righteousness and to rout the forces of
wickedness.

Zarathushtra conceives *Spenta Mainyu* as the son of
Ahura Mazda, the first in the creation, occupying the
first place in the celestial hierarchy. It is through him
that the Prophet longs to approach Ahura Mazda, and
it is through him that the human mind receives divine
illumination. Good thoughts proceed from him, and
good words and good deeds are the outcome of good
thoughts. At the opposite pole stands *Angra Mainyu*,
the Evil Spirit, who introduces discord and death in
the world. The *daevas*, the offspring of the Evil Spirit,
have chosen him as their lord; and he teaches them to
mislead man through evil thought, evil word, or evil
deed, and to lure him by his wiles to the path of
wickedness. Whoever falls a victim to *Angra Mainyu*
finds his thoughts enslaved by him. Man must avoid
him as he would a pestilence. The best way to avoid
the Evil Spirit is to think of and to espouse the cause
of the Good Spirit. It is only when man's mind is not
filled with good thoughts of *Vohu Manah* that it becomes
an easy prey to *Angra Mainyu*.

"From the regions of the North rushed forth *Angra
Mainyu*, the deadly, the *daeva* of the *daevas*, to lure
the Prophet away from the path of righteousness, but
he was met by the Holy One chanting the sacred formula *Ahunavar*. *Angra Mainyu* persuaded the Prophet
to renounce the law of God and held up to him the
temptation of sovereignty over nations. The Holy One,

however, turned away from him with a contemptuous
'No,' and crowned his victory over the Evil Spirit
with the prayer beginning with the words: 'This I ask
Thee: teach me the Truth, O Lord.' "* Every Zoroastrian believes that the best weapon he has at hand to
fight the Evil Spirit is the formula Ahunavar,† the
paternoster of Zarathushtra.

Man's Mission on Earth

Confronted by the two contending forces, how shall
man shape his course?

It is the wish of Ahura Mazda that His vicegerents
on earth should purify, renovate, and restore to its
pristine purity what is spoiled in creation by the Evil
Spirit. By going through the experience of good and
evil, by resisting evil and choosing good as their motto,
they have the opportunity of bettering their position
and raising their dignity in this world and the next.

Man is endowed with reason and free will. If he
brings evil on himself, it is because he yields to the
Deceiving Principle within him. When he thus deviates
from the moral law, he, as it were, strays away from
the abode of his real, or higher, self. He must either
resist and conquer evil, or submit and acknowledge

---

* Vendidad xix. 1–10.

† This is the most ancient text, and, therefore, the most difficult to
translate. We have almost as many versions as there are scholars. The
following rendering indicates the gist of it: "As there is a Supreme Lord,
so there is a Spiritual Chief by reason of his righteousness. The gifts of
Good Mind are for those working for the Lord; and the strength of
Ahura is given unto him who is a protector of the poor."

defeat. Imperfect is the world that man inhabits. In striving to render it perfect he is a fellow-worker with God. Whoever fights ignorance, fanaticism, falsehood, corruption, injustice, war, disease, and death, is God's ally in destroying the powers of imperfection. This combative view of life is the dominant note of Zoroastrianism. Redemption lies in co-operation with good and conflict with evil. In this the Prophet was following for the most part the ethics of his time. The power of love to cast out wrong had not as yet dawned on the world. Force was, therefore, to be met with force. Helping the wicked was tantamount to being wicked.

Exploded Theory of Dualism

This ethical doctrine of the two principles of good and evil gave rise in later years to the belief in cosmic dualism. *Spenta Mainyu* came to be identified with Ahura Mazda Himself, and such an identification engendered the belief that the world was created and governed by two deities, Ahura Mazda and *Angra Mainyu*, each independent of the other, the one good and the other evil; the one creator and the other destroyer; the one bright and the other dark; the one tending to the good thought, good words, good deeds, good aspirations, good intellect, good life and good religion, and the other tending to destruction, evil thought, evil words, evil deeds, unholy aspirations, evil intellect, evil belief, and evil religion. On the other hand, the Gathas and even some parts of the

later Avesta furnish positive evidence of the uncompromising monotheistic character of the creed as
preached by the sage of Iran. In all his utterances he
subordinates the two Spirits to Mazda, who mentions
them as "My Spirits." In the Gathas, Ahura Mazda is
the father of Vohu Manah, and therefore distinct from
him. In the nineteenth chapter of the Yasna, Ahura
Mazda says: "Of the two spirits, the Beneficent one
said to my whole tribe of the pure. . . ." Here, far
from being identified with *Spenta Mainyu*, Ahura Mazda
stands at a distance from him. Elsewhere in the same
sacred book it is distinctly stated that Ahura Mazda,
"desiring good, has created both weal and woe"
(Yasna xlv. 9).*

The Evil Spirit who disputes the kingdom on earth
with the Holy Spirit and introduces discord in the
world is the opponent not of Ahura Mazda but of
Spenta Mainyu. There is conflict between the two
spirits which seems everlasting, but which is bound to
end in the victory of the Good over the Evil Spirit.
The scriptures of the most optimistic living religion in
the world speak definitely of the ultimate triumph of
the Good Spirit and of the hiding of the Evil Spirit
underground. Ultimate victory of righteousness over
wickedness is thus the end of all earthly strife. The
twin spirits meet, in the words of Professor Jackson,
"in the higher unity of Ahura Mazda."

* Dhalla: *Zoroastrian Theology*. Cf. "Practically, however, Zarathushtra
treats Mazda as the only Creator and Supreme God . . . . Zoroaster is to
all intents and purposes a monotheist." *The Philosophy of the Good Life*.

Chapter XI

ESCHATOLOGY

MAN's composition, according to the system of Zoro-astrian religion, is of a triple character—material, vital, and spiritual—body, life, and soul. As his spiritual parts were created before his material and vital parts, they are undying. They combine with his physical parts at his birth and separate at his death. Of these spiritual parts the principal are *urvan*, the soul, and *fravashi*, the spirit, with their several faculties such as *manas*, the mind, and *bodha*, conscious-ness. The living body (*tanu*) is to the soul (*urvan*) and to the spirit (*fravashi*) what an instrument is to the worker, or a horse to the rider, or a house to its master. In this classification are discerned all the ele-ments of the modern tripartite division of man's per-sonality into reason, feeling, and will.

Preservation of one's health is one of the religious duties of a Zoroastrian. In his daily communion with God the devout Zoroastrian prays for "one thousand-fold health, ten thousandfold health."

It was believed that fasting militated against the maintenance of health and against the performance of good and great deeds. Fasting is, therefore, deprecated.

"This maxim should be borne in mind," says the *Vendidad*, "none of those who abstain from food is able to do great deeds of holiness, to do great works of husbandry, and to give birth to powerful children. The whole material world lives by eating; by fasting it dies."

The key to salvation lies as much in the purity of the body as in the purity of the soul. Hence the Zoroastrian dictum: *Yaozdao Mashyai aipi Zanthem Vahishta* (purity is the best from the very beginning of one's birth). Contact with impure matter in any form must be avoided. If contaminated, the body should be purified by means of various purification ceremonies prescribed by the scriptures. Such purification is imperative from the point of view of health as well as morals. Not only one's own body, but also the four elements, fire, air, water, and earth, must be preserved undefiled. It is also obligatory on a true Zoroastrian to keep his surroundings clean. Similarly, for the preservation of mental health, the religion of Zoroaster lays special emphasis on the triad—good thoughts, good words, good deeds. This fundamental doctrine of the creed takes the devotee down to the mainsprings of action. Thought is of no less importance than word or deed. The great triad not only establishes its parity with word and deed, but also gives it precedence as the source of all good words and good deeds

Free Will

Free Will is implicit in this doctrine of human personality. As man must work out his salvation himself, the Omniscient Lord, who plans what is best, has allowed him freedom to act. Exercising this freedom, man chooses between the principles of light and darkness, between truth and falsehood, between good and evil. Growing in mental vigour in the knowledge of the Law, ne acquires the kingship of self-control. Placing his will in harmony with the Law, he is able to withstand the assaults of falsehood and wrong, and cultivating the attributes of *Spenta Armaiti*, benevolence devotion, love, and social service, he attains the best state of the Most Perfect and Beneficent Spirit.

Reward and Punishment

Beyond the practical side of the religion of Zara-thushtra ranges its eschatology. The doctrine of reward and punishment in this life stretches onward into the next. The man who chooses the truth is here rewarded by Ahura Mazda with spiritual as well as temporal benefits. Thus the Prophet, who praised agriculture as the best weapon with which the demons of hunger and thirst, sickness and sorrow, theft and rapine, could be fought asks Ahura Mazda, for himself, whether he may have the reward of his labours in "ten mares, a stallion, and a camel," while he is assured salvation and immortality in the life to come.

Likewise, to a man who deserves happiness in the Future Life, he promises in this world a pair of cows with calf.

Despite the depressing spectacle of wrong and suffering all around him, Zarathushtra held fast to his conviction of the justice of God. The Omniscient cannot be so foiled as to allow wickedness to triumph over goodness. The Prophet, therefore, does not for a moment lose the vision of a better world. The perfect world is in the making. In it the balance will be redressed, the righteous made happy, the unrighteous chastised and purified. Zarathushtra is thus the first among the prophets of the great religions to preach the doctrine of immortal life.

The Soul's Equipment

The soul is responsible for deeds done in the flesh. According to the teaching of the Prophet, God has equipped man with every kind of appliance to perform his work successfully. For instance, he is endowed with *khratu*, energy, knowledge; *chisti*, consideration, wisdom; *ushi* (hosh), intelligence, perception, sense; *manas*, mind, thought; *vachas*, speech; *shyaothna*, action; *kama*, free will; *ahu* practical conscience; *fravashi*, the prototype in nature and in men, which is also the guiding spirit; *baodhas*, consciousness, memory. Over and above all these gifts is *daena*, the vision, the revealed religion.

Having been thus equipped, the human soul is

expected to emerge successful from the struggle with
the forces of evil. Man receives reward or punishment
after death according to his deeds. There is none to
intercede for him. No intercession will help him. No
amount of prayers and offerings will open the gates of
paradise for him. No particular creed or belief in any
set dogmas will save him from retribution. In short,
no trace of vicarious salvation can be seen in the
message of Zarathushtra. Man is his own saviour. He
has the making of his own Heaven or his own hell.
The small prayer *Vispa Humata, Vispa Hukhta, Vispa
Hvarshta*, which a devout Zoroastrian recites thrice in
the morning, reminds him that "a man's good thoughts,
good words, and good deeds lead him to Heaven; his
bad thoughts, bad words, and bad deeds lead him to
Hell." "As you sow, so shall you reap," is the maxim
writ large on page after page of the Yasna:

"Evil for evil, good reward for the good."
"Affliction to the wicked, happiness to the
   righteous."
"Woe to him who oppresses us (the righteous)!
"Woe to the wicked! Salvation to him who upholds
   righteousness!"

This is the quintessence of Zarathushtra's speculation
concerning life after death. No religious leader
before him had grasped the idea of guilt and merit
so clearly as he did.

The Ascent of the Righteous Soul

Man enters heaven or hell after death, according to the preponderance of his good or bad deeds. "One should prepare and carry provisions for the spiritual world from the material world," runs the admonition in the *Banam-i-Izad*, "so that the soul may not be in trouble." On the fourth day after death the soul has to cross the bridge, called *Chinvat*, which connects this world with the unseen world. Those righteous souls who have devoutly followed the precepts of Zarathushtra easily go over this bridge and enter heaven, whereas those that have turned themselves away from the Path of Righteousness stand trembling at this *judgment span*. Writhing with the anguish of their conscience and uttering words of woe, they are led by their own conscience to perdition, the Abode of the Worst Mind. The ascent of the righteous soul heavenward is allegorically described in the following passage:

At the close of the third night, when the dawn breaks, the soul of the righteous person passes through the trees, inhaling sweet fragrances; it seems as if a wind were blowing from the region of the South; from the regions of the South, of sweet fragrance, of sweeter fragrance than other winds.

And it seems to the soul of the righteous person as if it were inhaling that wind with the nose, and it thinks: "Whence does that wind blow, the wind of the sweetest fragrance that I ever inhaled with my nostrils?"

It seems to him as if his own conscience were advancing to him with that wind in the shape of a maiden, fair, bright, of white arms, courageous, beautiful, tall, with prominent breasts, beautiful of body, noble, of glorious birth, of fifteen years, and of a form as fair as the fairest of creatures.

Then the soul of the righteous person addressed her asking: "What maiden art thou, the fairest of maidens whom I have ever seen?"

Then replied unto him his own conscience: "O thou youth of good thoughts, good words and good deeds, and of good conscience, everybody loved thee for the greatness, goodness, beauty, sweet fragrance, courage, innocence, in which thou dost appear to me.

"Thou didst love me, O youth of good thoughts, good words, good deeds, and good conscience, for the greatness, goodness, beauty, sweet fragrance, courage, innocence, in which I appear to thee.

"When thou didst see others practising heresy and idolatry, causing harm and working destruction to plants; then thou wouldst sit chanting the holy songs, sacrificing unto the good waters and the fire of Ahura Mazda, and causing joy to the righteous coming from near and far.

"Lovely as I was, thou madest me more lovely; beautiful as I was thou madest me more beautiul; favoured as I was, thou madest me more favoured: seated as I was on an exalted place, thou madest me sit on a more exalted place, through thy good thoughts, good words, and good deeds; and so men will hereafter sacrifice unto me who have long sacrificed unto and have been in communion with Ahura Mazda."

The first step that the soul of the righteous person made, placed him in the Good Thought paradise; the second step that the soul of the righteous person made, placed him in the Good Word paradise; the third step that the soul of the righteous person made, placed him in the Good Deed paradise; the fourth step that the soul of the righteous person made, placed him in the Endless Lights.*

* Yasht 22, 7–15 (Dr. Dhalla's translation).

Such is the strictly rational and spiritual conception of heaven as the region of the best thought, or the best life. The modern Persian word for heaven is *behesht*. It is a later form of the Avestan word *Vahishta*, which is, philologically, nothing more nor less than the English word "best." Try to be *beh*, or good to-day; try to be *behter*, or better to-morrow, and try to be *behest*, or the best, the day after. These are the stepping-stones to the abode of the Good Mind. Be good, better, and best in your thoughts, words, and deeds, and you ascend to heaven. This, put in simple words, is Zarathushtra's philosophy of future life. Heaven and hell are not primarily the regions set aside for souls after death. Heaven is simply the best life or the region of best mental state, and hell the worst life or the region of the worst thought.

Between heaven and hell lies an intermediate place for those souls whose good deeds and evil deeds exactly balance. This is called the doctrine of *Hamestagan*; and it occupies a prominent place in the eschatological ideas of the later Pahlavi period. As Dr. Dhalla points out, the strict topic of the doctrine of Zoroastrian eschatology and the symmetry of the entire system demand a place where the souls that cannot ascend to heaven because of the heaviness of their sins, and yet all not so weighed down by sin as to descend into hell, can find their resting-place till the final judgment.*

* *Zoroastrian Theology.*

Chapter XII

THE FINAL DISPENSATION

BEYOND the hope of a future life for the individual there is the idea of a glorious consummation for the whole creation. The Gathas refer to a period when the present cycle of the world will be completed, the process of creation will cease, and the evolution of the Universe will have reached its destined goal. The world-process will then come to its final consummation as contemplated and ordained by Ahura Mazda at the dawn of creation. Then will arise the last of the saviours, Saoshyant. He will consummate the work of purifying and regenerating the world and completely removing every trace of the evil work of Angra Mainyu. All the souls of the wicked will be brought out from hell and lustrated and purified at the termination of their sentence. The souls of the righteous too will rise. There will thus be brought about the Ristakhez, i.e., the Resurrection

Renovation of the World

Thereafter, the world will enter upon a new cycle, free from all evil and misery, ever young, ever rejoicing, all souls enjoying a life of ineffable bliss and glory. "Then," it is said in the *Zamyad Yasht*, "he (the *Saoshyant*) shall restore the world, which will (thenceforth) never grow old and never die, never decay and never perish, ever live and ever increase, and be master over its wish, when the dead will rise, when life and immortality will come, and the world will be restored at (God's) wish." Thus will be consummated the triumph of *Asha*, or Righteousness, over *Druj*, or Wickedness.

What becomes of *Angra Mainyu*, the father of evil? His fate is not mentioned in the sacred books. One may infer, however, that when once the rule of evil perishes, its originator is rendered innocuous. The ultimate defeat of *Druj* necessarily implies the defeat of the *Arch-Druj*, *Angra Mainyu*.

Progress the Watchword of the Creed

Correspondence with the divine essence and purpose of God cannot be reached without the attainment of the highest state of perfection, but it was the hope of the Prophet that such a renovation of the world would come soon, even during his life. Progress, continuous progress, was the watchword of his creed. He was not unaware of the countless obstacles to progress that have to be encountered at every stage, but it was his conviction that although it might be retarded at times, progress could never be wholly arrested. A Zoroastrian is thus buoyed up with the belief that in the endless chain of Boundless Time human beings can contribute their share towards the establishment of the Kingdom of Righteousness on earth. None need feel appalled because he has to work in a circumscribed sphere. Nor need anyone be staggered at the vastness of the work to be accomplished. Each individual life should add something to the sum total of the life of humanity. Every one has to consecrate one's life and dedicate one's deeds to the good of humanity.

The Prophet's Message of Hope

This is the common aim that knits together man with man at all times and in all climes and will continue to unite those that will inhabit this world to the end of time. By the unceasing efforts of the ages and the accumulated achievements of humanity, the desired object will at last be secured. The great world drama will then be over; the final curtain will be drawn on the conflict between good and evil, the ultimate triumph of good over evil will be secured, the kingdom of Righteousness will be established, the good will live in a renovated world; and all this will come to pass through the exertions of man and his cooperation in this great task with his Creator. Thereafter, man will enter into the everlasting joy of Ahura Mazda.

Such is the message of Hope that the Prophet of

Iran has brought to this world from the Heavenly
Father.

"And this I ask Thee, O Ahura Mazda!
    The truthful righteous striving to further the well-
        being of his house, his province, and his
        country,
    How shall he be like unto Thee?

"When shall he be worthy of Thee?
    What actions of his shall most appeal to Thee?
    Clear is all this to the man of wisdom, as to the
        man who carefully thinks,
    He who upholds Truth with all the might of his
        power,
    He who upholds Truth to the utmost in his word
        and deed,
    He, indeed, is Thy most valued helper, O Mazda
        Ahura!

"To him, who is Thy true friend in spirit and in
        actions, O Mazda Ahura,
    To him Thou shalt give Healthful Weal and
        Immortality;
    To him Thou shalt give perpetual communion
        with Truth and the Kingdom of Heaven,
    And to him Thou shalt give the sustaining strength
        of the Good Mind.*

    * *The Divine Songs of Zarathushtra*, by D. J. Irani.

Chapter XIII

THE ZOROASTRIAN CODE OF ETHICS

THE fundamental principle of the creed is embodied in the triad *Humata, Hukhta, Hvarshta*, good thought, good word, good deed. The antithesis of this triad, which is the sum and substance of all morality, is *Dushmata, Duzukhta, Duzvarshta*, evil thought, evil word, and evil deed. '*To all good thoughts, words, and deeds (belongs) Paradise, so is it manifest to the pure.*'' This is the simple admonition given in the prayer *Vispa Humata*. In another prayer the devotee says: ''Henceforth let me stand firm for good thoughts, good words and good deeds, which must be well thought, must be well spoken and must be well done.''

Cultivation of Civic Virtues

Great importance was attached by the ancient Zoroastrians to the training of the youth in civics. They considered it essential so to educate children during their most impressionable days as to deepen their concern for the common good and to stimulate and diffuse a spirit of citizenship. In the *Cyropaedia* Xenophon gives an interesting account of the schools in Iran, in which such training was given, the first of the kind recorded in history.

"In every Persian city," says Xenophon, "is a free square, from which commerce and industry are rigorously excluded, and which contains the palace and the chief municipal buildings. On one side is the school for children from five to sixteen (up to five they live at home in the nursery), on the second, the institute for youth from sixteen to the full manhood of twenty-six, on the third, that for the man of mature years, on the fourth, that for the elders who are past the age of military service. The curriculum is remarkable; there appear to be no lessons, but only debates and 'trials' dealing with the practical events of the school life and conducted under the presidency of an appointed elder. These occupy the greater portion of the day; the rest is occupied with riding and shooting on the campus." As Xenophon puts it: "The Persians send their children to school that they may learn righteousness, as we do that they may learn letters."

Some of the notable virtues on which special emphasis was laid in the scriptures and which, one might expect, could not have failed to influence the life and character of the followers of the faith, may be noted.

Righteousness

Holiness, or righteousness, is a somewhat loose rendering of the Avestan term *Asha*; it gives but a faint idea of the original mystical and sublime conception of *Asha*, as embodied in the Gathas. In those hymns *Asha* is a profound spiritual truth, or a spiritual law in accordance with which the Universe has been fashioned and governed. All the earthly phenomena are to be traced to *Asha*. Man must obey this great law, for it is *Asha* that would lead him into the presence of Ahura Mazda. *Asha* is thus a very comprehensive term in Zoroastrian ethics. It signifies order, symmetry, discipline, harmony, and includes all sorts and acts of purity, truthfulness, and beneficence. The very first prayer that a Zoroastrian child is taught to recite is the aphorism, *Ashem Vohu*, which runs as under:

"Righteousness is the best of gifts and divine happiness. Happiness to him who lives for the sake of best righteousness!"

From order and discipline proceeds righteousness; from disorder and discord unrighteousness. *Asha* includes order; *Druj*, the opposite of *Asha*, signifies disorder. To uphold *Asha* at all times and in all circumstances is a duty enjoined on a true Zoroastrian. In fact all religious teachings begin with this alpha and omega of the creed. It is the Eternal Verity, the One Reality, which is the mainspring of all manifestation. Philologists have shown that phonetically this word *Asha* in the Avesta is identical with the ancient Vedic word *Rita*. The phonetic identity is, however, not so important as the striking identity of concept. *Rita* has exactly the same significance as *Asha*, showing that this one fundamental conception of the progress heavenwards is common to the philosophy of all Indo-Iranian peoples. It is this law, this path of *Asha* (*Ashahe Pantao*) or *Rita* (*Ritasya Pantha*) by which man may hope to reach the Father in Heaven.

"I am on the side of those who preserve order, not on that of those who create disorder," says Ahura Mazda in the *Hom Yasht*.

"There is but one Path," we are warned in the *Yasna*, "the Path of *Asha*; all other paths are false paths."

What reward awaits the man who treads this Path is exquisitely indicated in the following verse of the *Hush bam* (the Dawn Hymn):

"O Ahura Mazda! grant that through the best *Asha*, through the most perfect *Asha*, we may catch sight of Thee, we may approach Thee, we may be united with Thee!"

Thus *Asha*, purity, leading from bodily health and vigour to mental and spiritual health and strength, is the most sublime elaboration of the conception of cleanliness being next to godliness. Not only is cleanliness next to godliness, but it is also in itself a form of godliness.

Man pleases Ahura Mazda by practising truth.

"Let us reach the paths of truthfulness, wherein abides Ahura Mazda, through his Holiness," prays a devout Zoroastrian. It is said in *Gatha Ushtavaiti*, "Whoever shows the beneficial paths of truthfulness (to another) in this corporeal world, wherein is the abode of Ahura Mazda, attains supreme good fortune.''

Many a classical author refers with approbation to the systematic manner in which the virtue of truthfulness was cultivated among the ancient Iranians. "Beginning from the age of five years to twenty," said Herodotus, "they instruct their sons in three things only, to ride, to shoot with the bow, and to speak the truth." "To tell a lie," says the same author, "is considered by them the greatest disgrace; next to that, to be in debt; and this for many other reasons, but especially because they think that one who is in debt must of necessity tell lies."*

Justice

Justice, according to the *Avesta*, goes with truthfulness. Hence, *Arshtat*, or *Ashtad*, the Yazata who presides over truthfulness, is often an associate of *Rashnu*, the Yazata presiding over justice. On the Judgment Day, the fourth day after death, when the soul of the deceased is judged by *Mener Davar*, that dispenser of justice is helped in his work by *Arshtat* and *Rashnu*. In his daily prayers a Zoroastrian invokes *Rashnu* in these words:

"We invoke the truthfully spoken word. We invoke righteous obedience. We invoke noble righteousness. We invoke the words which impart manliness. We invoke the victory-giving peace. . . . We invoke

* Cary's translation, p. 61.

truth which brings about prosperity to the world, and benefit to the world, and which is (the chief characteristic of) Mazda-yasnan religion. We invoke the most truthful *Rashnu*" (Visparad vii. 1, 2).

"A truly uttered speech," it is said in the *Sarosh Yast Hadokht,* "is the most victorious in assembly." Declaring that true evidence and justice are pleasing to God, the Gathas exhort the devotee to cultivate the virtue of impartiality and justice. "Fight your cause by fair means even with your enemies," is another injunction. So great is the estimation in which justice is held that a holy, just, and impartial judge is compared to Ahura Mazda and to the Ameshaspends, and an unjust judge to Ahriman and the *Daevas.*

Similarly, good government, according to the *Minokherad,* is that which designs and directs that the city may be prosperous, its poor relieved from hardship, and which repeals unjust laws and rules and promulgates laws and ordinances that are just and fair.

The *Meher Yasht* begins with the following exhortation to be faithful to one's pledge. "The man guilty of being untrue to his pledge is guilty of an act tantamount to injuring the whole country. Do not, therefore, break a plighted pact, be it made with an *Asho* or a *Darvand,* for both are vows alike; it does not matter whether a pledge is given to a *Darvand* or to one of your own ways."

Similarly, the Yasna insists on faithful discharge of one's debts. "In all (dealings) debts must be paid with true thought, true word, and true deed to the men to whom they are due.''

Chastity

Sanctity of wedded life is one of the virtues insisted upon in the religion of Zarathushtra. It demands, from husband and wife alike, ''devotion to the Good Mind and holiest deeds of fidelity.'' What is heinous in woman is equally loathsome in man. The Zoroastrian code of ethics thus places both the sexes on a level unparalleled in the history of Asiatic people.

''Him, O Pouruchista, thou of the family of Haechataspa and Spitama, youngest of Zarathushtra's daughters, has he (the Prophet) chosen as thy husband, him who is devoted to the Good Mind, Righteousness, and Mazda. Counsel then with him with thy wisdom and do with good intent the holiest deeds of devotion.''

''Unto maidens marrying, I speak words of monition and unto ye bridegrooms, lay them to heart, wise with precepts, strive for the life of the Good Mind that the home-life of each shall be happy'' (*Yasna* 53, 3, 5).

The woman who keeps her feet constantly in the path of chastity is assigned the exalted rank of a *Yazata*. ''The righteous woman, rich in good thoughts, good words, and good deeds, well-instructed and accomplished, obedient to her husband and chaste, and such as Aramaiti (Devotion) the bounteous is, and

such as other female Yazatas are" (Gah. iv. 9). On
the other hand, the woman who strays from that path
is reprehended as worse than a viper or a she-wolf.
There is no place for a courtesan in the social organiza-
tion of the Zoroastrians. "Her look dries up a third
of the mighty flowing waters; her look takes away a
third of the growth of the blooming, beautiful, green-
coloured trees, her look takes away a third of the
verdure of the bountiful earth, her touch takes away
a third of the courage, victory, and truthfulness of a
righteous person of good thought, good words, good
deeds. Therefore, I say unto thee, O Spitama Zarathushtra, that such a one is more deserving of death
than gliding snakes, or howling wolves, or the prowling
she-wolf that falls upon the fold, or the she-frog that
rushes into the water with her thousandfold brood"
(*Vendidad* xviii. 63–65).

Self-help

As a practical religion, Zoroastrianism lays particular emphasis on self-help, industry, and dignity of
labour.

"With self-help one becomes independent" (*Yasna*
9, 25).

"I shall chase away Sloth, which makes one lean.
I shall chase away Sloth, the long-handed" (*Vendidad*
xi. 9).

"Arise, O men, praise the best purity, smite down
the *daevas*. Otherwise, the long-handed Sloth, who

lulls the whole material world to sleep, again will rush towards you as soon as the day breaks and men are wide awake. O men! it does not behove you to sleep for a long time" (*Vendidad* xviii. 16).

"Eat of your own regular industry" (*Ashirwad*).

"No harm to the honest and the industrious, living among the wicked" (*Yasna* 19, 6).

"Never, O Mazda! shall the deceitful lazy have a share of the good creed" (*Yasna* 31, 16).

Whoso Sows Corn Sows Righteousness

"Creator of the material world, Thou righteous one! What is the way for furthering the Mazda-Yasnan religion?"

To this question Ahura Mazda replies:

"Incessant cultivation of corn, O Spitama Zara-thushtra! Whoso cultivates corn cultivates righteousness; he advances the Mazda-Yasnan religion with a hundred feet, he suckles the Mazdayasnan religion with a thousand breasts and strengthens it with ten thousand offerings."

In these words of profound philosophical significance the Sage of Iran preached the gospel of work—work as opposed to sloth, industry as opposed to and as an antidote for destitution and degradation.

Idleness is the parent of want and shame. It invokes the demons of hunger and thirst, sickness and suffering, dependence and disease.

"Whoso does not till this earth
With the left arm and the right,
With the right arm and the left,
Then unto him says the earth, 'O thou,
Who dost not till me
With the left arm and the right,
With the right arm and the left,
Verily shalt thou stand,
Leaning at the door of the stranger
Among those that beg for food;
The refuse, indeed, for thee
Will they bring as food,
Those who have profusion of good things.' "

The chief weapon with which one could have fought the fiends of hunger and thirst in the days of Zarathushtra was agriculture, the only important industry of the age. It is said in the *Vendidad*:

"When corn grows the demons start in dismay: when the sprouts are out, the demons cough; when the stalks are seen, the demons shed tears; when the ears are out, the demons take to their heels; in the house where the corn is turned into flour, the demons are smitten:

"It seems as if it turned
Red hot iron in their jaws
When corn is stored in plenty."

Care of Cattle

In words typical of the pastoral age the Prophet pays homage to the cow: "Praise to the cow, good words to the cow, victory to the cow, food and pasture to the cow! Let us work for the kine, for they yield us our food! (*Yasna* 20).

Care for and maintenance of *gospend*, innocent and useful domestic animals, such as cows, goats, sheep, and dogs, is a virtue specially inculcated by the Prophet of Iran.

"May we be one in spirit with the Behman Ameshaspend of good mind," prays the devout Zoroastrian, "who spreads peace in the midst of good creation. Animals of all kinds in the world are under his protection. Those, from whom these animals get food, maintenance, and protection, and are well-clothed. Sufficient vesture clothes them."

"Whoever wishes to propitiate *Vohu Manah* (the Ameshaspend presiding over Good Mind and over the animal creation) in the world and wishes to act for his happiness is he who wishes to promote the things of Vohu Manah; it is necessary for him, so that Vohu Manah may be ever with him, that he should propitiate, at every place and time, the well-yielding cattle in whatever has happened and whatever occurs and should act for their happiness; and in the terrible days of troubled times which befell them, he should afford them protection from the oppressive and idle. He should not give them as a bribe to a man who is a wicked tyrant, but should keep them in a pleasant and warm locality and place; and in summer he should provide them a store of straw and corn, so that it is not necessary to keep them on the pastures in winter. . . . He should not drive them apart from their young, and should not put the young apart from their milk. Since they are counterparts of him (Vohu Manah) in this world, the well-yielding cattle, whoever propitiates those which are well-yielding cattle, his fame subsists in the world, and the splendour of Ahura Mazda becomes his own in the best existence'' (*Shayast la Shayast*, xv. 9–11).

Compassion

Compassion is mentioned as an attribute and crowning glory of the strong. "The mightiest in the mightiest, becoming the throned monarch better than his crown, an attribute of God Himself."

Zarathushtra asks Ahura Mazda: "How are we to worship Thee and Thy *Amesha-Spenta*?"

Lord Almighty replies: "He who desires to please Ahura Mazda in this world, must desire to develop (i.e. to further the increase of) the creation of Ahura Mazda. It is necessary that the person to whom Ahura Mazda is attached should please the righteous by relieving suffering and protecting them from the evil-minded (*Pahlavi Rivayet* attached to the *Shayast la Shayast*, xv. 3 and 7).

Charity

In the list of the positive virtues which a follower of Zarathushtra is expected to cultivate, charity takes the foremost place. It is one of the fundamental precepts of the creed.

"He who gives succour to the helpless poor, acknowledges the kingdom of God" (*Ahunavar*).

"O Mazda! What is your Kingdom? What is your Will, by acting according to which I may come unto your friendship?"

Ahura Mazda replies: "You will come unto my friendship by helping your poor fellow-men who live righteously and with good mind" (*Gatha Ahunavad. Yasna 24, 5*)

"Ye Zoroastrian Mazdayasnans! Hold your hands and feet steady. . . . Relieve those who have fallen in distress" (*Visparad* xv. 1).

"Grant me . . . a child . . . that relieves distress" (*Atash Nyaesh, Yasna 62, 5*).

Another invocation in the *Yasna* runs:

"May, in this house, generosity triumph over stinginess!"

It must, however, be judicious and discriminating charity. While it is meritorious to extend one's bounty towards deserving objects, it is reprehensible to extend it to those who are unworthy of it.

Miserliness is reprobated. "He who, though quite able, does not readily give in charity, shall go to destruction without attempting to avert it."

"He who is without charitable feeling in him . . . let torment freely come to him,"

There is no place for the selfish and the sordid in the Zoroastrian fraternity. The prayers and offerings of such persons are not acceptable to God. "I will not accept," says Lord Almighty in the *Aban Yasht*, "the offerings proffered to me by . . . wicked, cruel, selfish persons."

Promotion of Education

Charity consists not merely in relieving distress and satisfying the physical wants of those around us, but also in ministering to their intellectual, moral, and spiritual wants. The religious books of the Parsis, therefore, emphasize the duty of providing facilities for the education of all men and women, married or single, virtuous or vicious. It is a specially meritorious act to help those who are in need of help to be educated.

"If men here come as co-religionists or brethren or friends . . . to seek knowledge . . . let those who seek for knowledge, be given that knowledge with holy words . . ." (*Vendidad* iv. 44).

"He who desires the light of knowledge desires the gifts of an Athravan (spiritual teacher). He who desires for the fullness of knowledge, desires the gift of an *Athravan*" (*Zamyad Yasht* liii).

The reference to the *Athravan* may be read with the following verse from the *Vendidad*:

"Him thou shalt call an *Athravan*, O holy Zarathushtra, who throughout the whole night seeks for
joy-producing knowledge which delivers him from
affliction, which bestows comfort at the Chinvat
Bridge, which obtains for him the desires of the world,
which makes him attain to purity, and which makes
him attain to the best thing of the best Existence
(Paradise)."

"Do not keep your wife, children, co-citizens,
and your own self without education, so that grief
and misery may not befall you and you may not
have cause to repent" (*Pand-Namah-i Adarbad Maraspend* xiv).

"Which is the highest of all deeds of men?"

The answer to this poser in the *Dinkard* is: "To give
knowledge to those who are fit to receive it and to
give birth to every kind of holiness."

In another Pahlavi text, the *Sikand-Gomanik-Vijar*,
it is said: "One who, from the little knowledge which
he has given to those who are fit for it, is more acceptable than he who, though he knows, yet does not
profit or help deserving persons."

That epithet "deserving" introduced in the later
injunctions should not be taken to exclude sinners.
The Prophet of Iran emphasized the duty of correcting
and improving those that had been lured away from
the Path of Righteousness. The best service a man
can render to society consists not merely in one's
own virtuous conduct and deeds, but also in bringing
about a reform in society by the dissemination of

knowledge among the members thereof, virtuous and vicious alike.

It is said in the *Yasna* that he who tries to check the activities of a man of vicious tendencies by instructing him, after chastising him, offers a love-service acceptable to Ahura Mazda.

"He who chastises the vicious either by word, or by thought, or by both the hands, and who giveth instruction to that vicious person in anything that is good, such persons are devoted unto the Will of Ahura Mazda according to the pleasure of Ahura Mazda."

The duty of ministering to the moral and spiritual needs of one's fellow-citizens, thus enjoined, cannot be lightly overlooked. No matter how virtuous a man may be, if he ignores this paramount obligation, eh shall have to pay the penalty for it on the day of judgment. Says the *Bundehesh*: "Every body will see (the consequence) of his good actions or evil actions At the end, in the midst of the Anjuman, the sinful will be conspicuous in the same way as a white sheep is conspicuous in the midst of black sheep. In that assembly a sinful person will thus complain against his or her righteous friend in this world who failed to lead him to the path of righteousness: 'Why did you not teach me to perform the virtuous deeds which you performed?' The righteous man shall then have to quit the assembly, much discomforted for having neglected the duty."

Service and Beneficence

A good deed is superior to ten thousand recitals or prayers.

"Be most beneficent," runs the exhortation in *Afrin-e Buzorgan*, "as is the Lord Ahura Mazda to His creations." Similarly, the *Visparad* inculcates the gospel of service and sacrifice:

"Be ready with your feet, hands, and understanding, O Mazdayasnan Zarathushtrian, for the prompt discharge of good, fitting, and timely deeds, for the avoidance of inappropriate and untimely wicked deeds. Be alert to accomplish in this world good deeds and to afford help to the helpless and the needy."

According to the admonition given in the *Banam-i-Izad*, a Zoroastrian should render unto himself an account of his daily deeds. Before retiring every day he should carefully ask himself and ponder over these questions: "How many good deeds have I done to-day; how many good deeds am I able to perform? How many bad deeds have I committed; how can I abstain from sin?"

Practical Philosophy of the Creed

Such is the practical morality and philosophy of Zoroastrianism. It is to these doctrines of piety and truth, industry and self-help, compassion and charity, humanity and service, that the survival of the faith of Zarathushtra till this day as the Religion of the

Good Life is due. One of the most elevating marriage benedictions is *Hukerdar bed chun Hormazd pa daman-i-Khesh*, meaning "Be a doer of good deeds as Ahura Mazda is to His own creation." This is in keeping with the entire tenor of the philosophy of Zarathushtra's creed, which makes correspondence with the character and purpose of God the essence of the good life for man.

"BE LIKE GOD!" These are the three words in which the entire philosophy of life may be summed up. Likeness to God is the only way of communion with the Heavenly Father. There is no other path to Heaven.

Chapter XIV

WORSHIP

In the teachings of Zarathushtra, as embodied in his *Gathas*, there is hardly any mention of the ritual of worship. No offerings; no sacrifices; only the heart's yearnings and the soul's striving are the gifts demanded of the devotee. This is all the more remarkable as the orthodox form of worship in ancient Iran included animal sacrifices and offerings to the *daevas*.

In consonance with the teaching of the Prophet, the devotion of his followers merely takes the form of fervent exaltation of moral and spiritual ideals and an ardent desire for the cultivation of such ideals. The very first prayer that a Zoroastrian child is taught to recite is *Ashem Vohu*, a very brief prayer in praise of *Asha*, or righteousness. This is one of the sacred formulae of great importance, spoken of as *Mathra Spenta* in the Avestan texts. There are many such spells of varying degrees of efficacy, but the greatest of all, the Word *par excellence* of the Zoroastrian theology, the most excellent, the most mighty, the most efficacious, the most healing, the most smiting, and the most victorious, is the *Ahuna Vairya*. It is made up of twenty-one words, every one of which corresponds to one of the Nasks, which make up the complete Holy Writ of the Zoroastrians. Of all the sacred formulae that have ever been pronounced, or are now recited, or will hereafter be recited, this Word which Ahura Mazda Himself pronounced when the world was not, and which He announced to the Holy Prophet, is the best. It is, in fact, the quintessence of the entire scriptures. A single recitation of it earns for the worshipper merit equivalent to that of singing a hundred Gathas. Zarathushtra himself repelled the Evil Spirit, when the latter tempted him, by chanting aloud the same Word of mysterious power.*

Homage to Ahura Mazda

"Through good mind and through rectitude and through the deeds and words of wisdom, we come near unto Thee. Unto Thee we pay our homage, and we acknowledge ourselves Thy debtors, O Mazda Ahura! With all good thought and with all good words and with all good deeds we come near unto Thee."

"As Thou, O Ahura Mazda, hast thought and spoken, decreed and done what is good, so do we give unto Thee, praise Thee, and worship Thee. Thus do we pay homage unto Thee and acknowledge ourselves Thy debtors."

"Grant, O Mazda, for this life and the spiritual

* Vide p. 101, ante (Chapter x).

life, that we may attain to fellowship with Thee and righteousness for all Time.''

"Unto Thy good kingdom, Mazda Ahura, may we attain for ever. In both the worlds, O most Wise One among beings, art Thou the good king of us, men and women. We dedicate ourselves unto Thee, of good renown, the adorable one, the possessor of truth; therefore, O most Wise One among beings in both the worlds, be Thou unto us our life and body. May we deserve and obtain, O Mazda Ahura, lifelong joy in Thee! May we love Thee and lean upon Thee for strength. O most Wise One among beings, cheer us and make us happy for all time!''

"So Zarathushtra gives, as an offering, even the life of his body and the excellence of good thought unto Mazda, and willing obedience and power of deeds and words unto righteousness.'

"And this will we choose for ourselves, O Mazda Ahura, and O beautiful Asha! that we think, speak, and do deeds that are the best of all deeds for the world. By reason of the rewards for these best deeds, we will strive, both lettered and unlettered, rulers and servants, to give rest and fodder to the cattle. Evermore we will, so far as in us lies, keep possession of and impart to other. the rule of the best ruler and prepare it, namely, the rule of Mazda Ahura and Asha Vahishta. And as every one knows clearly—man or woman—so shall one do for oneself according to one's best knowledge that which is good, and further teach it to those who should do it as the case may be. Since we reckon as the best, offering of worship and homage to Ahura Mazda and the feeding of the cattle, that we do and also teach others to do to the best of our ability. In the rule of Asha and amongst the people of Asha, there is for every man the best life as reward in both the worlds. And these, Thy revelations, O Ahura Mazda, we will propagate with the best thought of Asha."

"Grant me that, O Mazda, which will be a source of joy to Thee!"

"May we be the seekers of Mazda's rejoicing and may we pay our homage to Him with humility!"

"O Mazda Ahura! Lifting up my hands in all humility to Thee, who are Invisible and Munificent, I pray with joy for righteous actions, for benevolent thoughts, so that I may thereby rejoice the Soul of the Universe!"

The following are some of the daily prayers, or extracts therefrom:

Confirmation

"Victory to the truest and holy religion of divine knowledge made by Mazda!

"Triumph of the good Mazdayasnian Zoroastrian Faith!

"That's the good, righteous, and unpolluted religion, which Ahura Mazda has sent to this world, and which is brought to us by Zarathushtra, the Prophet.

"The Zoroastrian Faith of Ahura Mazda is granted to Zarathushtra for his Righteousness.

"Righteousness is good, righteousness is the best."

Morning Prayer

"Hail! O Dawn! Hail to Thee!
Hail! in order to sacrifice all that is greatest to
    Him
Who is Ahura Mazda,
The Corporeal as well as the Spiritual Lord.
In order to crush the evil Angra Mainyu,
To destroy the demon of Anger, deadly armed;
To crush the devils of Mazandaran;
To annihilate all evil spirits.
We here respectfully remember all pious Men
    and Women of all the World,
All that are, and were and are to be."

Night Prayer

"We respectfully here remember the Angel Sraosha,
The holy and the beautiful,
The earthly promoter and the victorious holy
    lord.
We remember him, who, himself awake, protects
    the creations of Ahura; who, himself awake,
    preserves the creatures of Mazda.

We remember him, who fights against the devils
of Mazandaran, all day and night.
We remember him, who is the Protector and
Supervisor of the World."

The Path to the Lord

"O Holiness! when shall we see thee,
And thou Good Mind, as we discover
Obedience, the Path to the Lord,
To Mazda, the most beneficent?
With that Manthra we will teach
Foul heretics faith in our Lord.
Come with the Good Mind and give us
Asha-gifts, O Thou eternal!
Grant that to us by whose aid
We may crush the evils of the evil."

"We Praise These!"

"We praise the intelligence of Ahura Mazda, in order
to grasp the holy word.
We praise the wisdom of Ahura Mazda, in order to
study the holy word.
We praise the tongue of Ahura Mazda, in order to
speak forth the holy word.
We adore, every day and night, the mount Ushi-
darena, the Giver of Intelligence.
Beloved of Gaokerena made by Mazda, we praise
him the more, more than any other of the Pious."

Ideal Man and Woman

"We praise the pious Woman, well-versed in good thoughts, words, and deeds, well-educated, honouring the husband, holy and bounteous like Spenta Aramaiti and Thy other female Yazatas, O Ahura Mazda!

We praise the pious Man, well-versed in good thought, words, and deeds, steadfast in piety, and 'the holy lord of the ritual.' "

"Work is Worship"

"Hold ready, O Mazdayasnian Zoroastrians! Your feet, your hands, and your intelligence;

In order to perform good deeds, according to the Law and at the right time.

In order to avoid bad deeds, which are not according to the Law and are done at the wrong time.

Let us set our feet in industrial pursuits.

And place above want those that are needy."

PART TWO

RITUAL

Chapter I

SOCIO-RELIGIOUS CEREMONIES

Birth Ceremonies

"I PREFER," says Ahura Mazda in the *Vendidad*, "a person with children to one without children." Even the soil feels happy where a man with children lives. This conviction makes the advent of a child doubly welcome in a Zoroastrian home. We do not find in the Avesta any reference to pregnancy rites In the later Pahlavi and Persian books, however, we find references to certain rites. For instance, the *Sayast la Sayast* directs that during the days of pregnancy a fire may be maintained most carefully in the house. According to the *Vendidad*, the place for delivery must be very clean, dry, and least frequented by others. After delivery, the mother should avoid contact with fire, water, and the *baresman* (i.e. the sacred ceremonial apparatus) of the house. It enjoins a period of twelve days for such isolation in the case of a still-born child.

Marriage Ceremonies

After prolonged contact with the Hindus in India, the present-day followers of Zarathushtra have adopted several Hindu marriage customs and ceremonies, but the strictly religious part of the ceremony, as performed by the officiating priests, is more or less orthodox Iranian and is conducted mainly in the later Pazand language. It consists of :

(1) Preliminary benedictions.
(2) Questions to the marrying couple and the witness on either side.
(3) Joint address by the two officiating priests.

The senior priest blesses the couple in these words: "May the Creator, the Omniscient Lord, grant you a progeny of sons and grandsons, plenty of means to provide yourselves, abiding love, bodily strength, long life for a hundred and fifty years."

Thrice during the course of the benediction a declaration of the witnesses and of the bride and bridegroom is taken by the priest. The witness on behalf of the bridegroom's family is first asked:

"In the presence of this assembly that has met together in the city of —— on —— day of —— month of the year —— of the era of Emperor Yazdagard of the Sassanian dynasty of auspicious Iran, say, whether you have agreed to take this maiden —— by name, in marriage for this bridegroom, in accordance with the rites and rules of the Mazdayasnans, promising to pay her 2,000 *dirams* of pure white silver and two *dinars* of real gold of the Nishapur coinage."

"I have agreed," replies the witness.

Then the following question is put to the other witness: "Have you and your family with righteous mind, and truthful thoughts, words, and actions, and for the increase of righteousness, agreed to give for ever this bride in marriage to ———?"

He replies: "We have agreed."

The priest then asks the couple: "Have you *agreed* to enter into this contract of marriage (and abide by it) till the last day of your life, with a righteous mind?"

Both reply: We have *agreed*."

Then follows the recital of the *Paevandanama*, or *Ashirwad*, an address replete with benedictions, admonitions, and prayers, by the two officiating priests who keep on showering on the couple grains of rice as an emblem of happiness and plenty.

The *Ashirwad* is not merely a benedictory address; it is also a little sermon which closes with a short prayer. Likewise, the admonitory part of it is not merely a homily exhorting the bride and the bridegroom to cultivate good qualities, to do good and to shun evil; it is also a discourse for the entire assembly on worldly wisdom and a key to success in life. As an illustration, the following extracts may be noted:

"Do not quarrel with the revengeful. Never be a partner with an avaricious man. Do not be a comrade of a back-biter. Do not join the company of persons of ill-fame. Do not co-operate with the ill-informed. Do not enter into any discussion with persons of bad report. Speak in an assembly after mature consideration. Speak with moderation in the presence of kings."

"Oh, ye good men," says the officiating priest,

"may good accrue to you as the result of perfect good thoughts, perfect good words, and perfect good deeds! May that piety come to you which is the best of all good. May not sinful life, which is the worst of all evil, come to you. . . . Righteousness is the best gift and happiness. Happiness to him who is righteous for the sake of the best righteousness!"

In the concluding paragraph of the *Ashirwad* the married couple is blest in these terms:

"May they have light and glory, physical strength, physical health, and physical success; wealth that may bring with it much happiness, children blest with innate wisdom, a very long life and the blissful paradise, which is due to the pious! May it be so as I wish it!"

Funeral Ceremonies

It will be convenient to treat the funeral ceremonies and observances under the following two heads:

(1) Ceremonies relating to the disposal of the dead.
(2) Ceremonies relating to the soul.

Disposal of the Dead

To maintain fire, air, water, and earth pure and undefiled is a cardinal principle of the Zoroastrian creed. It is enjoined that the body of a person, after the soul has left it, should with due respect to the deceased be disposed of in such a manner as not to defile these elements or to injure the living. Accordingly, the followers of the creed do not burn or bury their dead, or consign them to the water. They merely expose the dead, on the top of a high hill, to the heat of the Sun, there to be devoured by carnivorous birds. Their funeral ceremonies are likewise based on the ancient Zoroastrian ideas of sanitation, segregation, and purification. All the ceremonies of this order appear to have anticipated the prophylactic measures taken in modern times for the prevention of epidemics, namely, (1) breaking the contact of the living with the real or supposed centre of infection, and (2) destroying such a centre itself. As a matter of precaution, all cases of death are treated as infectious, and the followers of the faith are warned that they should bring themselves, as little as possible, into contact with dead bodies.

Soon after death, the corpse is washed and a clean suit of clothes is put over it. The Kusti, or the sacred thread, is then put round the body with a prayer. The corpse is placed on the ground in a corner of the front room on large slabs of stone, or impermeable, hard, dry clods of earth. The hands are folded upon the chest crosswise. After the corpse is placed on slabs of stone, one of the two professional corpse-bearers, to whom the body is entrusted, draws round it three *Kashas*, or circles, with a metallic bar or nail, thus reserving temporarily the marked plot of ground for the corpse so as to prevent the living from going near it and catching infection.

The dead body is then shown to a dog with two eye-like spots just above the eyes. It is believed that this particular kind of spotted (*Chathru Chasma*, literally, "the four-eyed") dog has the faculty to detect whether life in the body is extinct or not. It is expected to stare steadily at the body, if life is extinct; but not even to look at it if otherwise.

Fire is then brought into the room in a vase and is kept burning with fragrant sandalwood and frankincense. Before the fire sits a priest who recites the Avestan texts till the time of the removal of the corpse to the Tower, and keeps the fire burning. The corpse may be removed to the Tower at any time during the day, but not at night, as the body must be exposed to the Sun.

About an hour before the time fixed for the removal of the body to the Tower, two or, if the body is heavier, four *Nassasalars*, i.e. corpse-bearers, clothed completely in white, enter the house. In the case of a death due to an infectious disease, all the exposed parts of the body, except the face, are covered up, so as to prevent infection through any uncovered part. They carry a bier, called *gehan*, invariably made of iron, to remove the body. Wood being porous and, therefore, likely to carry and spread germs of disease and infection, its use is strictly prohibited in the funeral ceremonies.

The corpse-be   place the bier by the side of the corpse. They then recite in a suppressed tone the following formula of grace, and remain silent up to the time of the final disposal of the corpse in the Tower of Silence.

"(We do this) according to the dictates of Ahura Mazda, according to the dictates of the Amesha-Spenta, according to the dictates of the Holy Sraosha, according to the dictates of Adarbad Maraspend, and according to the dictates of the Dastur of the age!"

They sit silent by the side of the corpse. If there is any occasion on which they must break silence, they do so in a subdued tone, without opening the lips.

Then follows the "Geh-Sarna" ceremony, i.e. the recital of the *Gatha*, which is intended to be an admonition to the survivors to bear with fortitude the loss of the deceased. After this, the corpse is again shown to the dog; the relatives and friends, who have by this time assembled at the house, then have a last look of the deceased. After the *geh-sarna* ceremony, the mourners pass, one by one, before the corpse, to have a last look and to bow before it as a mark of respect.

The corpse-bearers then cover the face with a piece of cloth and secure the body to the bier with a few straps of cloth. They carry the bier out of the house and entrust it to the *Khandias*, another set of corpse-bearers, whose business it is to carry the bier on their shoulders to the Tower.

When the bier reaches the Tower, it is put on the ground outside; the corpse-bearers uncover the face, and those who have accompanied the funeral procession pay their respects and have a last look from a distance of at least three paces. After the dead body is once more exposed to the sight of the "four-eyed" dog, for the last time, the gate of the Tower is opened. The *Nassasalars*, who took the corpse out of the house and have accompanied the corpse to the last resting-place, now take over the bier from the carriers and take it into the Tower, and place the dead body on the space set apart for it. They then tear off the clothes from the body of the deceased and leave it on the floor of the Tower. Naked one comes into this world; naked one leaves it.

The body is exposed and left uncovered, so that the eye of the flesh-devouring birds may be drawn to it. The sooner it is eaten up, the fewer the chances of further decomposition, and the greater the safety of the living. The clothes removed from the corpse are thrown in a pit outside the Tower, where they are destroyed by the combined action of heat, air, and rain. In Bombay they are destroyed with sulphuric acid.

On completing their work the corpse-bearers lock the Tower. Thereupon an attendant claps his hands as a signal to all those who have accompanied the funeral procession and who have by this time taken their seats at some distance from the Tower. They all get up from their seats and recite the rest of the *Sraosh baj* prayer, of which, before joining the procession, they had recited only a part. This is followed by a short prayer, in which they say: "We repent of all our sins. Our respects to you (the souls of the departed). We remember here the souls of the dead who are the spirits of the holy."

The Tower of Silence

"O Holy Creator of the Material World! Where are we to carry the bodies of the dead? O Ahura Mazda! Where are we to place them?" asks Zarathushtra in the *Vendidad*.

Ahura Mazda replies: "O Spitama Zarathushtra, on the most elevated place."

In the earliest times corpses were exposed on the summits of high mountains without any inclosures. When the bones were denuded of flesh by dogs, vultures and other carnivorous birds, and rendered absolutely dry, and desiccated in the course of a year. they were removed and preserved in *Astodans*, that is, receptacles for the preservation of bones, the stone-urns referred to by classical authors. The *Astodans* were made of stone, mortar, or any other durable substance capable of withstanding infection, as the means of the relatives of the deceased permitted. The existing Towers of Silence are so constructed as to secure the ready disposal of the flesh and the preservation of the bones; and it is recognized that the modern method is superior to the ancient, inasmuch as it does not involve defilement of a large area of ground and recognizes no distinction between the rich and the poor. All bones are disposed of in the same well, establishing equality of all in death.

The Bombay Towers of Silence

The best example of the modern method is to be seen in the Bombay Towers of Silence. It is a round, massive structure, built entirely of solid stone. A few steps from the ground lead to an iron gate which opens on a circular platform of solid stone with a circular well in the centre. The circular platform inside the Tower, about three hundred feet in circumference, is paved with large stone slabs, well-cemented, and divided into three rows of shallow, open receptacles, corresponding to the triad, good thought, good word, good deed. The first row is used for corpses of men, the second for corpses of women, and the third for corpses of children.

There are footpaths for corpse-bearers to move about. A deep central well (*bhandar*) in the Tower, about one hundred and fifty feet in circumference (the sides and bottom of which are also paved with stone slabs), is used for depositing the dry bones. The corpse is completely stripped of its flesh by vultures within an hour or two, and the bones of the denuded skeleton, when perfectly dried up by atmospheric influences and the powerful heat of the tropical sun, are thrown into this well, where they gradually crumble to dust, chiefly consisting of lime and phosphorus.

In the compound of the Tower, at a short distance from it, there is a small building called *sagri*, where a sacred fire is kept burning day and night. In *mofussil* towns, where it is not possible to do so, at least a light is kept burning.

Ceremonies relating to the Soul of the Deceased

"O Ahura Mazda, Beneficent Spirit, Holy Creator of the material world! when a pious man dies, where dwells his soul for that night? . . . Where for the second night? . . . Where for the third night?" asks Zarathushtra in the *Hadokht Nask*.

Ahura Mazda replies: "It remains at the place of his body, singing the *Ustavaiti Gatha*, asking for blessedness: 'Blessedness to him whom Ahura Mazda of His own will grants blessedness!' "*

If it is the soul of a wicked man, it remains within the precincts of this world for three nights. Remembering all the sinfulness of its past life and feeling at a loss where to go, it clamours: "Oh, Ahura Mazda! To what land shall I turn? Where shall I go?"

The soul of a dead person that thus remains within the precincts of this world is under the special protection of Sraosha, whom Ahura Mazda has appointed to guard the souls of men during life and after death. The religious ceremonies for the soul of the dead during the first three days are, therefore, performed in the name of, or with the propitiatory formulae of invocation (*Khshnuman*) of, Sraosha. The *Shayast-la-Shayast* enjoins: 'During all the three days, it is neces-

* Vide Haug's Texts and Translation in the Book of *Arda Viraf*, pp. 309-10.

sary to perform the ceremony (*Yazisn of Sraosha*) because Sraosha will be able to save his soul from the hands of the *daevas* during the three days; and when one constantly performs a ceremony at every period (*gah*) in the three days, it is as good as though he should celebrate the whole religious ritual at one time."

At the commencement of every *gah*, two or more priests and the relatives of the deceased recite the *Sraosh baj* and the formula of the particular *gah*, and the *patit*, or the penitence prayer, with the *Khshnuman* of Sraosha. At night two priests perform the *afringan* ceremony in honour of Sraosha. They sit on a carpet face to face, with an altar of fire and a metallic tray between them. The senior priest, who has the tray before him, is called the *Zaotar*, or invoking priest. The other, who has the altar of fire before him, is called the *Atarevaks*, or the nourisher of fire. The metallic tray contains a pot of pure water and a few flowers.

The Zaotar begins the Afringan, invoking in the course of the introductory portion, which is composed in the Pazand language, the protection of Sraosha upon the soul of the deceased, who is specifically mentioned by name in the prayer. Both the priests then recite together the seventh section of the *Sraosha Yasht*, which sings the praises of the *Yazata* for the protection it affords.

Besides these prayers and ceremonies, which are performed for three days and nights at the house of the deceased, the *Yasna* litany, and, sometimes, the *Vendidad* with the *Khshnuman* of Sraosha, are recited at an adjoining fire-temple for three successive mornings and nights.

The Uthamna Ceremony

In the afternoon of the third day, a ceremony is performed, called the *uthamna*, before an assemblage of friends and relatives of the deceased and a few priests. The special prayer prescribed for this period of the day, namely, the *Sarosh Hadokht* and the *Patit*, are recited, also a Pazand prayer with the *Khshnuman* of Sraosha, wherein the name of the deceased is mentioned and the protection of Sraosha is implored for him. This is an occasion for announcement of charities. At the end of the ceremony, the relatives and friends of the deceased generally announce donations to charity funds in the *nivat*, or memory, of the deceased.

Passage of the Soul to the Other World

On the dawn after the third night the soul is believed to pass on to the other world, crossing the bridge called *Chinvat*. This bridge is guarded by the Yazata *Mithra*. "When the third night ends and the day breaks, with the first appearance of light in the morning, the well-armed Mithra appears on the Elysian heights.* This Yazata, who is known in the

* *Vendidad* xix. 28.

later books as *Meher Davar*, i.e. Meher the Judge, is assisted by *Rashnu*, the *Yazata* of Justice, and *Astad*, the *Yazata* of Truth. They judge the man's actions during his-life time. If his good deeds outweigh the bad ones even by a small particle, his soul is allowed to pass over the bridge to Paradise; if his good deeds just balance his misdeeds, the soul goes to a place called *Hamestagan*;* but if his misdeeds outweigh his good deeds, even by a particle, he is flung deep down into the abyss of hell.''

The dawn after the third night after death is, therefore, regarded as a very important and solemn occasion for the performance of religious ceremonies for the benefit of the soul of the deceased. The ceremonies performed in the afternoon on the previous day are repeated; the *Afringan* and *Baj* prayers are recited, and other ceremonies are performed. This being the day of judgment, the relatives and friends of the dead join in prayer for God's mercy on his soul.

Baj ceremonies are recited, firstly in honour of the *Yazata Rashnu* and *Astad* together, who help the *Yazata Meher*; secondly, in honour of *Rama Khvastra*, who is the Yazata presiding on the rarefied atmosphere, or ether; thirdly, in honour of *Ardafravash*, i.e. the holy spirits of all the departed souls, whom the deceased has joined; and fourthly, in honour of *Sraosha*, who guided the soul of the deceased in its journey to the other world. When the *Baj* of *Arda-*

* *Vendidad* xix. 36.

fravash is recited, a suit of white clothes, together with the sacred bread and other votive offerings, is consecrated by the priest. This suit of clothes is called *syav*. It is the *vastra* mentioned in the *Fravardin Yast*: "Who will praise us . . . with clothes in hand?"* This suit of clothes is generally given as a gift to the priest or to the poor. The other principal occasion, on which the *Afringan-Baj* ceremonies should, according to the scriptural injunctions, be performed in honour of the dead, are the *Cheharum*, *Dahum*, *Siroz*, and *Salroz*, i.e. the fourth day, the tenth day, the thirtieth day, and the anniversary day.

Death does not put an end to the relation between the deceased and the surviving members of his family. According to the Zoroastrian belief, the holy spirit of the dead continues to take an interest in the living. If the surviving relatives cherish his memory, remember him with gratitude and try to please him with pious thoughts, pious words, and pious deeds the departed spirit takes an interest in their welfare, and assists them with invisible helping hands. Therefore, the most essential tribute with which a surviving relative can please the holy spirits of his departed dear ones consists of pious thoughts, words, and deeds. Thus the performance of meritorious and charitable deeds constitutes a connecting link between the living and the dead. The scriptures praise "the brilliant deeds of piety in which the souls of the deceased delight";† and on the days dedicated to the memory of the

---

* Frav. Yast. xiii. 50.   † *Yasna* (Ha xvi. 7).

deceased, their relatives not only remember them and pray that their souls may rest in peace, but also distribute food and clothing among the poor of their community, and, if they can afford it, set aside various sums in charity.

Chapter II

PURIFICATION CEREMONIES

Yaozdao mashyvai aipi zahythem vahishta (Purity is the best from the very beginning of one's life). This oft-repeated saying in the scriptures brings home to a Zoroastrian the sublimity of purity. Purification is held essential from the view-point of health as well as morals. As the mind is believed to receive some sympathetic aid from the purity of the body, and as cleanliness influences one's moral character, purification of the body is invariably regarded as an emblem of purity of the mind.

Men and women coming in contact with impurities must purify themselves, not only for their own good, but also for the good of others. It is not enough that they should keep their bodies clean; all household articles and utensils likely to have been defiled should also be purified. Even though they may not have come into actual contact with impurities, should there be the slightest suspicion that they have been affected in some way, they should, as a matter of precaution, purify themselves by means of various kinds of ablutions, accompanied in certain cases by segregation and performance of ceremonies. These purificatory ceremonies are divided into four categories: (1) *Pad-yab*; (2) *Nahn*; (3) *Bareshnum*; and (4) *Riman Si-shoe.*

Padyab

The *padyab* is the simplest form of purification of the exposed parts of the body. The word literally means "throwing water (*ab*) over (*naiti*) the exposed parts of the body." The person performing the *padyab* says at first *Khshnaothra Ahurahe Mazdao*, i.e. "I do this to rejoice Ahura Mazda." Then he recites the short formula of *Ashem Vohu* and washes his face and the other exposed portions of his body, hands, and feet. He then wipes his face and the other parts of the body and finishes the process by performing the ceremony of *kusti*, which consists of untying and re-tying the sacred thread with the recital of certain formulae.

There are four occasions on which a Parsi has to perform the *padyab*: (1) early in the morning after rising from his bed, (2) after answering calls of nature, (3) before taking his meals, and (4) before saying his prayers.

Nahn

Nahn, bath, is a higher form of purification gone through on specified occasions with the help of a priest. It consists of four parts: (1) the ordinary *padyab-kusti*; (2) the chewing of a pomegranate leaf and the drinking of the consecrated *gomez*, or bull's urine, a sort of symbolic communion; (3) the recital of the *patit*, or prayer of repentance; and (4) the final bath.

After performing the *padyab*, the man going through the ceremony recites the *baj*, or prayer of grace recited before meals, and chews one or two leaves of the pomegranate tree. given to him by the priest. He then performs the *Kusti*, recites the *Patit*, and then goes through the *nahn* proper. Retiring to a bath-room, he recites the *Kshnaothra Ahurahe Mazdao* formula, undresses himself, recites a part of the *Sraosh baj*, placing his right hand over his head, as praying with an uncovered head is prohibited. The priest hands him from outside, in a long spoon tied at the end of a stick having nine knots, various articles believed to have purifying properties. Thrice he hands him the conse-crated urine, which is rubbed over the body three times. Then, he gives him thrice a little quantity of sand, which also is rubbed over the body. Next, he is given thrice the consecrated water, which, too, is rubbed over the body thrice. A few drops of the sacred water are generally sprinkled over the new suit of clothes to be put on after the bath. He then bathes with water which has been hallowed before-hand with a few drops of the consecrated water. After completing his bath, he puts on the consecrated suit of clothes, finishes the *Sraosh baj* prayer, and performs the *kusti*. This finishes the *nahn* purification.

Orthodox Zoroastrians usually go through this form of purification on the occasion of the *Naozot*, the ceremony of investing a child with the sacred shirt and thread, and on the occasion of marriage. Women go through it at the end of their period of accouchement, while some devout persons resort to it on the occasion of the Farvardegan, the sacred days at the end of the year.

Bareshnum

This is the highest form of purification. The original object was to purify those who had been in contact with the worst forms of impurity, which appeared to be dangerous or infectious. In ancient Iran a man who became unclean by contact with the dead, or through any other source of defilement, was required to go through this course of purification. When death occurred from an infectious disease, those who had been in contact with the dead and were, therefore, likely to spread contagion, had to subject themselves to *purification* and *segregation* for nine days. As a matter of precaution, it was also enjoined that the living should, for a time, keep themselves away from the dead body, whether death was due to an infectious disease or not; and that those who, for one reason or another, could not help remaining in close contact with the dead, should go through the long form of *bareshnum* purification and segregation.

Bareshnum differs in several respects from the two rites already described. While the *padyab* takes one or two minutes, and the *nahn* about half an hour, the *bareshnum*, which originally had the object of both purification and segregation, lasts nine days. While the *padyab* needs no help of a ministe·, the *bareshnum* requires the services of two priests. While the first two ceremonies can be performed in any ordinary house or in a temple, the *bareshnum* purification must be gone through in a place open to the sky and set aside for the purpose, where there is no vegetation, water, or fire, likely to be sullied by the touch of the defiled person undergoing the purification.

In modern times it is only the priests and initiates who go through this ceremony. It is incumbent on a person who wishes to be initiated into the priestly profession, as well as on a full-fledged priest who wants to officiate within the inner circle of the fire-temple at some of the superior functions of ritual, to go through this form of purification.

Si-Shoe

In recent times persons defiled by contact with dead bodies are required to go through a comparatively simpler form of purification known as *Si-shoe*, i.e. thirty-times washing. For the performance of this rite the services of two persons are required, of whom one must be a priest. The materials for purification and the processes of the baths are almost the same as in the case of the *rahn* purification.

Chapter III

INITIATION CEREMONIES

THERE are two initiation ceremonies: (1) The *Naozot*, being the initiation of a child into the Zoroastrian society, and (2) the *Navar* and the *Murattab*, the two grades of initiation into the priesthood.

The Naozot

The ceremony of investing a child with the sacred shirt, called *sudreh*, and the sacred thread, called *kusti*, is known as *Naozot*. A Zoroastrian is free to dress as he likes, but after initiation, he must always, save while bathing, put on the *sudreh* and the *kusti* as symbols of Zoroastrianism. The word *naozot* means "a new invoker," and the ceremony is so called as it is only after its performance that a Zoroastrian child is under an obligation to offer prayers and to observe religious customs and rites.

The seventh is the usual year for a child's *naozot*. On the day fixed for the investiture, a few minutes before the time of the ceremony, the child is made to go through the *nahn* (ablution) ceremony, and then taken to a room where friends and relatives and priests have assembled. There the officiating priest sits with folded feet upon a carpet spread on the floor and the child is made to sit in front of him, with a sheet of white cloth round its body. The following articles, are laid on the carpet: (1) a tray containing a new suit of clothes for the child, including a *sudreh* and a *kusti*; (2) a tray of rice, which at the end of the ceremony is presented to the family priest; (3) a tray of flowers, which are presented at the end of the ceremony to the assembled priests, friends, and relatives; (4) a lamp, fed generally with clarified butter; (5) fire, burning on a censer with fragrant sandalwood and frankincense; (6) a tray containing a mixture of rice, pomegranate grains, raisins, almonds, and a few slices of coconut, which are sprinkled over the head of the child by the priest whilst giving his benediction. In the first tray containing the suit of clothes there are also some betel leaves and areca nuts, a few pieces of sugar, a few grains of rice, a coconut, a garland of flowers, a metallic cup containing *kunkun* (a kind of red powder), and a few coins. These things are not necessary for the ceremony proper, but they are regarded in India as emblems of good luck, and as such are presented by the priest to the child. At the end of the ceremony the coins are given to the family priest as part of his fee.

When all the priests have taken their seats, the officiating priest places in the child's hand a new shirt. They all then recite the *Patit*, the atonement prayer, or the *Hormazd Yasht*. The child also joins in reciting the prayer or its selected sections; generally, it recites in lieu thereof the *Yatha Ahu Vairyo* prayer. The officiating priest then rises from his seat and the child stands before him.

The first part of the investiture consists in presenting to the child the sacred shirt. This prayer is made up of two parts; (*a*) The Avesta *Khshnuman* of the *Yazata Din*, who presides over religion, and (*b*) the Pazand formula of the Confession of Faith. The confession, made up of these two parts, runs as follows:

"Praised be the most righteous, the wisest, the most holy and the best Mazdayasnian Law, which is the gift of Mazda. The good, true, and perfect religion, which God has sent to this world, is that which Zarathushtra has brought. This religion is Zarathushtra's religion which Ahura Mazda communicated to holy Zarathushtra."

On the child publicly making this declaration of its faith in the Zoroastrian Mazdayasnian religion, the priest clothes it with the sacred shirt. While putting it on, he chants the sacred formula of *Yatha Ahu Vairyo*, and the other priests join him. He then stands with the back of the child turned to him; facing the east if it is morning, and the west if it is evening, and recites the introductory part of the *Hormazd Yasht* and the *Nirang-i-Kusti*. The substance of this prayer is as follows: "The Omniscient Lord keeps back Ahriman powerless. May Ahriman with all his accomplices be smitten, vanquished, and dejected! Oh! Omniscient Lord, I repent of all my sins; I repent of all the evil thoughts that I may have harboured in my mind, of all the evil words that I may have uttered, of all the evil deeds that I may have done. The propitiation of Ahura Mazda and condemnation of Ahriman are the uppermost wish of those who work for the Truth.''

An elaborate process of girdling the *kusti* round the waist is then gone through. During the investiture of the sacred thread, the child recites, along with the officiating priest, the *Nirang-i-Kusti*, containing the last and the most important part of the Articles of Faith. "Oh! Almighty Lord! Come to my help! I am a worshipper of Mazda. I am a Zoroastrian worshipper of Mazda. I praise good thoughts, good words, and good deeds. I believe in the good Mazdayasnian religion, which cuts short discussions and quarrels, which is the dedication of the self, which is holy, and which of all the religions that are, that have yet flourished and are likely to flourish in the future, is the greatest, the best, and the most excellent, and which is the Ahurian Zarathushtrian Religion. I ascribe all good to Ahura Mazda. This is the creed of the Mazdayasnian faith.''

At the conclusion of the ceremony the officiating priest makes a red *kunkun* mark on the child's forehead—a long vertical mark if it is a boy or a circular mark if a girl— and places in its hands the coconut, flowers, and other articles mentioned above. There only remains then the recital of the *Tandarusti*, or benediction, by the officiating priest, who invokes the blessings of God upon the new initiate, in these terms:

"May you enjoy health, long life, and splendour of piety! May the good Yazatas and Ameshapands come to your help! May the religion of Zarathushtra flourish! Oh, Almighty God! May you bestow long life, joy, and health upon the ruler of our land, upon the whole community and upon this child! May the child live long to help the virtuous! May this day be auspicious, this month auspicious, this year auspicious! May you live for many a year to lead a holy, charitable, and religious life! May you perform righteous deeds. May health, virtue, and goodness be your lot! May all your good wishes be fulfilled by the Bountiful Immortals! Amen! Amen!"

Initiation into the Holy Order

Only the son of a priest can become a priest. To be a thoroughly qualified priest, he must go through two grades of initiation; (1) the *Navar*, and (2) the *Murattab*.

The Navar

One newly initiated into the work of offering prayers, rites, and sacred things to Ahura Mazda is called *Navar*. The candidate for initiation must first pass through two *bareshnum* purifications. He is then initiated into the order by two priests. To qualify themselves for the performance of the ceremony, these priests have to go through the *Gewra* ceremony, which consists of the performance, for six mornings, of the Yasna ceremony. On the sixth day of the *Gewra* ceremony, the priest who has on that day performed the *Yasna* ceremony initiates the candidate. The neophyte takes his bath with all its formalities and puts on a new suit of clothes, and is led to the fire temple in a procession. In a thickly inhabited city like Bombay the procession is formed in the temple itself. The neophyte then puts on the full ceremonial dress, wears on his shoulders a shawl and carries a *mace* (*gorz*) as the insignia of dignity and authority. When the procession arrives at the place of initiation, the candidate removes his full dress, lays aside the insignia of authority, and, under the guidance of one of the officiating priests, presents himself before the assembly. The initiating priest then asks the assembly. "Is it your pleasure that this candidate may be admitted?" After waiting for a few seconds for a reply, he takes the silence of the assembly to signify its will and consent, and expressing his pleasure gives his own consent. The candidate is then taken to the *Yazishn-gah*, i.e. the place set aside for the liturgical service, where he performs the *Yasna* ceremony and, subsequently, the *Baj* and *Afringan* ceremonies These are repeated for four days. After this, he is declared qualified to be a priest.

"The Zoroastrian *Navarhood*," says Dr. Modi, "in some of its features, reminds us of the Christian Knighthood of olden times, when Knighthood was a kind of religious order."

The points of similarity are the following: (1) The
Iranian *Navar* and the Christian Knight had each to
go through ceremonial baths. (2) Both had a white
dress as a symbol of purity. (3) The Knighthood had
its fasts; the *Navarhood* enjoined no fast but a kind of
abstention, or temperance. (4) Both had some weapons
to serve as symbols; the Knight had a sword; the
Navar a *gorz*, or a mace. (5) Both the orders signified
renunciation and a desire to serve and fight against
evil.

The Murattab

The priest who has gone through the *Navar* ceremony can perform only a few liturgical services; he
cannot officiate at the higher services performed in
the temples. In order to qualify himself to direct such
ceremonies, he must go through the second grade of
initiation and become a *Murattab*, that is, one who has
acquired the rank (*martabeh*) of a director of the priesthood. In this ceremony the initiate goes through the
bareshnum ceremony for ten days. On its termination,
he performs the *Yasna* ceremony on the eleventh day.
Thereafter, he is fully qualified to officiate as a
directing priest at all the ceremonies.

Chapter IV

CONSECRATION CEREMONIES

Consecration of the Sacred Fire and Fire Temples

There are three grades of Sacred Fires: (1) the *Atas Behram*, (2) the *Atas Adaran*, and (3) *the Atas Dadgah*. These three have their different rituals of consecration and also different rituals for the daily prayers during the five periods (*gahs*) of the day, when they are fed with fresh fuel.

The various processes for the consecration of the Sacred Fire of the *Atas Behram* are:

(1) Collection of the sixteen varieties of fire.

(2) Their purification.

(3) Their consecration.

(4) Their unification into one Sacred Fire.

(5) The consecration of the united Sacred Fire.

(6) Consecration of the Chamber of the Fire, the *sanctum sanctorum* of the Fire Temple.

(7) Enthroning the Sacred Fire.

Significance of the Processes

What does a Fire thus collected, purified, consecrated and enthroned signify? A Zoroastrian standing before the Sacred Fire thinks for himself: "When this fire on this vase before me, though pure in itself, though the noblest of the creations of God, and though the best symbol of the Deity, had to undergo certain processes of purification, had to have its essence, nay its quintessence of purity, drawn out to render itself worthy of occupying this exalted position, how much more necessary, more essential, and more important is it for me, a poor mortal prone to commit sins and crimes and to be contaminated with hundreds of evils, both physical and moral, to undergo the process of purity and piety, by making my *manashni*, *gavashni*, and *kunashni* (good thoughts, good words, and good deeds) pass, as it were, through the sieve of piety and separating by that means my *humata*, *hukhta*, and *hvarshta* (good thoughts, good words, and good deeds) from my *dushmata*, *duzukhta*, and *duzvarshta* (bad thoughts, bad words, and bad deeds), so that I may deserve an exalted position in the next world?"

The different varieties of fire are collected from the houses and places of business of men of different grades of society. They include even fire used in cremation or incineration, and the ceremony reminds a Zoroastrian that just as all the fires from the houses of men of different status have, by the process of purification, acquired without any discrimination the exalted place in the vase, so also before God men of all strata of society are equal, provided they pass through the process of purification and preserve purity of thought, purity of speech and purity of action.

When a Parsi goes before the Sacred Fire, the officiating priest holds before him in a ladle in his hand
the ash of a part of the burning fire. The devotee
applies it to his forehead, just as a Christian applies
the consecrated water, and thinks to himself: ''Dust
to dust. The Fire, all brilliant, shining, and resplen-
dent, has spread the fragrance of the sweet-smelling
sandalwood and frankincense round about, but is at
last reduced to dust. So is it destined for me. Let
me, like this fire, do my best to spread, before my
death, the fragrance of beneficence and the light of
righteousness and knowledge!''

Feeding the Sacred Fire

The ceremony of feeding the Sacred Fire in a fire
temple five times (*gah*) during the day varies according
to the grade of the Sacred Fire. In the case of the Fire
of the first grade, the priest must be one who has gone
through the *bareshnum* and has performed the *khub*
ceremony. After saying his prayers, he places some
frankincense and six pieces of sandalwood over the
fire in the form of a *machi*, or throne. He goes round
the censer, with a metallic ladle in his hand, and,
standing in eight different positions, the four sides and
four corners, recites different parts of a prayer, the
substance of which is as follows: ''Oh! God! We
praise Thee through Thy fire. We praise Thee by the
offering of good thoughts. We praise Thee through
Thy fire. We praise Thee by the offering of good

deeds. (We do all this) for the illumination of our thoughts, for the illumination of our words, and for the illumination of our deeds.''

Whilst uttering the words *dushmata, duzhukhta, duzvarshta* (evil thoughts, evil words, and evil deeds) during the recital of the first *Nyaesh* and the first *Pazand* portion thereof the officiating priest rings thrice the bell within the holy precincts of the altar of Fire. Some priests ring the bell thrice, whilst uttering each word, to emphasize that portion of the prayer in which the worshipper expresses his determination to shun bad thoughts, bad words, and bad deeds.

The ceremonies for the consecration of the sacred fires of the second and third grades are similar but simpler, and the number of different fires required for the purpose is smaller. The *boe* ceremony for feeding the fires is also simpler.

The temples, or buildings which hold the Sacred Fires, are consecrated with the recital of *Yasna, Vendidad, Afringan,* and *Baj* prayers for four days.

Consecration of the Towers of Silence

In the centre of the spot chosen for the Tower, a priest performs the *Baj* ceremonies in honour of Sraosha, the guardian-spirit guiding the souls of the dead, of Ahura Mazda, of Spenta Armaiti, the Amesha-spend presiding over the land, of Ardafravash, i.e. all the departed souls, and of *Haft Ameshaspend,* the seven Beneficent Immortals.

A few days later, two priests perform, in the morning, the *tana* ceremony for laying the foundation of the Tower. The ceremony is so called, as a very fine thread (*tana*) is used to make out the circumference of the Tower and its different parts for laying the foundation. A hundred and one fine threads are woven into one strong thread or string. The thread so prepared is required to be long enough to go thrice round the circumference and the inner parts. Some time before its use, this thread is made *pav*, i.e. washed, purified, and dried. To hold this thread, the priests have to drive in the ground three hundred and one nails of different sizes and weights.

In the central well of the Tower, called the *Bhandar*, two priests perform, for three consecutive days, the *Yasna* and *Vendidad* ceremonies in honour of the *Yazata Sraosha*, who protects the souls of the dead for three days and nights after death. On the morning of the fourth day, the opening day of the Tower, a *Yasna* ceremony is performed in honour of *Ahura Mazda*. Then the *Baj* and *Afringan* ceremonies are performed in honour of *Ahura Mazda*, of *Ardafravash*, i.e. the departed souls, of *Spendarmad*, i.e. the archangel presiding over mother earth, a portion of which is now occupied for laying out the dead, and of *Sraosha*. In the *Afringan* ceremony, known as the *Jasan* ceremony, which is performed in the presence of a large number of the community assembled to witness it, the name of the donor at whose expense the Tower is built is mentioned and the blessings of God invoked upon him. When the ceremony is over, the Parsis assembled throw into the central well of the Tower gold, silver, or copper coins, or even rings and other ornaments which help to make up the sum necessary for building the Tower, if it is built at the expense of the community. If, however, it is endowed by a donor, the amount thus collected goes to the head priest of the district in whose ecclesiastical jurisdiction the Tower lies. Sometimes he donates it to charitable trusts of the town.

Chapter V

LITURGICAL CEREMONIES

THERE are two kinds of liturgical ceremonies and services: the inner and the outer. The inner liturgical ceremonies and services are those which can only be performed in a place specially allotted for the purpose, known as the *Dar-i-Meher* (i.e. the House of Mithra), generally attached to a fire-temple. Under this head are included (1) the *Yasna* or *Yazisna*, (2) the *Visparad*, (3) the *Vendidad*, and (4) the *Baj* ceremonies.

The Yasna

The *Yasna* (Sanskrit, *Yajna*, or *Yagna*) is a prayer which includes the praise of God and His Spiritual Intelligences and invokes their aid. It is an extensive prayer with an elaborate ritual, in the course of which certain things are presented as symbols. Recital during the ceremony of all the 72 chapters, known as the *Has* of the *Yasna*, is a *sine qua non*.

The Visparad

The *Visparad* is a form of prayer intended to celebrate the season festivals; it is also a prayer wherein all the *ratu* or the chief or the best of creations are invoked. "The celebrations of the *Visparad*," adds Dr. Modi, "should suggest to the celebrant the idea of 'Excelsior.' " How is that state of "Excelsior" to be attained? The reply given in the *Visparad* is:

"Zarathushtrian Mazdayasnans keep your feet, hands, and understanding steady for the purpose of doing proper, timely, charitable works, and for the purpose of avoiding improper, untimely, uncharitable works. Let industry be your motto here. Help the needy and relieve them from their needs!"

The Vendidad

The *Vendidad* embodying the Law, as distinguished from the ways of the *daeva*, or the evil spirits, contains regulations and instructions, as to how best to withstand the evil influences of the *daeva*, or the forces that lead to the impurity and decay of body and mind. One part of it may be called the sanitary code, and the other the criminal code of the ancient Iranians.

The Baj Ceremony

The *Baj* ceremony, forming part of the funeral services after death, is performed on various occasions in a Zoroastrian house. The first three days after death are the principal days when these ceremonies are performed. The subsequent occasions are *chaharum*, or the fourth day, *dehum*, or the tenth day, *Siruz*, or the thirtieth day, and *Salruz*, or the anniversary.

It is the duty of the son, or the nearest heir of the deceased, to perform the *Buj* ceremony, wherein certain things which serve as symbols of the different kinds of creation, such as animal or vegetable creation, are submitted as offerings, a tribute either to the glory of the particular *yazata*, or heavenly being, or to the memory of a particular deceased relative.

The Outer Liturgical Services

These are ceremonies which may be performed in a *Dar-i-Mehr* as well as in any private residence, or place, and by any priest. These Outer Liturgical Services are known as (1) the *Afringan*, (2) the *Farokhshi*, and (3) the *Satum*.

The Afringan

Expressive of praise to God and the Higher Intelligences, the *Afringan* prayer corresponds to the *Apei* of the Brahmans. A fire is kept burning in a censer before the officiating priest and is fed with sandal-wood and frankincense. The offerings consist principally of fruit, flowers, milk, water, wine, and *sherbet* (syrup).

The Farokhshi

This prayer is intended to remember, invoke, and praise the *Fravashis* of the dead. Like the *Afringan*, it is generally recited over fruits, flowers, milk, wine, water, etc., and before fire. The *fravashi* is that power, or spiritual essence, in a substance, which enables it to grow. It is the spirit inherent in every thing, inanimate or animate, which protects it from decay and enables it to grow, flourish, and prosper. Every object in nature is believed to have its *fravashi*.

These *fravashis* are a kind of prototypes, and are analogous to the "ideas" of Plato who believed that everything had a double existence, first in idea and secondly in reality. According to the *Fravardin Yasht*, their number is legion, and they are spoken of as protecting and looking after the sea *Vourukasha* (Caspian). The same number looks after the constellation of *Haptoirang* (Ursa Major), the body of Keresaspa, and the seed of Zarathushtra. As the Universe is made up of innumerable objects, animate or inanimate, large or small, and as each object has its own *fravashi*, or some individual inherent spiritual essence which maintains and supports it, it is evident that there are innumerable such spirit essences, all emanating from that great Divine Essence of God who has created them, and who has made use of them.

Ahura Mazda is the Great Architect of the Universe. He is the Creator of the Material as well as the Spiritual world. The *fravashis* form the creation of the spiritual world. In the spiritual hierarchy, they stand, as it were, fourth in the order of supremacy.

Ahura Mazda (The Omniscient, Self-existent Lord) is at the head of all; next come the *Amesha-Spenta*

(The Bountiful Immortals), who are His own creations; then the *Yazatas* (*lit.* those who are worthy of being worshipped); and the *Fravashis* (i.e. the guarding or protecting spirits).

Zoroastrianism preaches veneration for the dead. It is believed that he dead have a future existence somewhere and that there exists some relation between the dead and the living. The channel, through which the relation continues, is the *fravashi*, or the guiding and guardian-spirit of the dead, who come to the help of the living, provided they live a pure and virtuous life and hold the departed ones in veneration.

Farokhshi is the recital of the praise of these *fravashis* in honour of the dead. It consists of the recital of the *Satum* prayer and the *Fravardin Yasht*. The offerings are the same as in the case of the *Afringan*.

Satum

This is a prayer in praise of the *fravashis* of the dead, generally recited over meals. The meal of the day is served in a tray and placed before the priest during its recital. The name of the dead, in whose honour it is specially recited, is mentioned first in a Pazand prayer.

Combined Groups of Liturgical Ceremonies

There are certain groups of ceremonies which are performed by celebrating a number of different liturgical ceremonies. Among such groups of services are the following:

(1) The *Homayasht* (The Haoma worship).

(2) The *Geti-kharid* (A corruption of the original Avestan name, *Usefriti*, the ceremony for seeking salvation from the sins of the world).

(3) The *Sraosh* (Funeral ceremonies performed in the honour of a deceased person during the first three days after death).

(4) The *Zindeh-ravan* (The *Sarosh* ceremony performed in one's lifetime).

(5) The *Gahambars* (Celebration of season festivals).

(6) The *Jashan* (Celebration of an important event or occasion).

(7) The *Frawardegan* (Ceremony in honour of the *fravashis*, or the guardian-spirits).

(8) The *Faresta* (Ceremony wherein all the Yazatas are invoked).

In the performance of these ceremonies the *Yasna, Vendidad, Visparad, Afringan, Baj,* and other prayers and ceremonies are gone through several times in specific order.

It will be observed that these observances and ceremonies are interwoven with the daily life of the followers of the faith of the great Prophet who preached his gospel of purity and perfection, devotion and benevolence three thousand years ago. How far the injunctions of the creed are in general agreement with the discoveries of modern science may be gathered

from the foregoing account of the rites and ceremonies enjoined by it. Indeed, if there is any religion
in which promotion of spiritual bliss as well as concern for material happiness ot mankind have been
blended in a remarkable degree, it is the faith of
Zarathushtra. Whilst dealing with the eternal problems
of life in a spirit pre-eminently human and rational,
and inculcating intense contemplation of and reverence
for the great beneficent works of the Creator and un-
swerving adherence to the principles of truth and
righteousness, this ancient religion lays down a code
of social purity based on sanitary and hygienic notions,
anticipating in many respects the teachings of modern
science.

INDEX